CLASS STRUGGLE
IN
AFRICA

ALSO BY KWAME NKRUMAH

BOOKS

Ghana: an Autobiography
Towards Colonial Freedom
I Speak of Freedom
Africa Must Unite
Neo-Colonialism
Challenge of the Congo
Axioms
Dark Days in Ghana
Voice from Conakry
Handbook of Revolutionary Warfare
Consciencism

PAMPHLETS

What I Mean by Positive Action
The Spectre of Black Power
Ghana: The Way Out
The Struggle Continues
Two Myths
The Big Lie

KWAME NKRUMAH

Class Struggle
in
Africa

INTERNATIONAL PUBLISHERS
NEW YORK

Published by Panaf Books Ltd., London, and
by International Publishers Co., Inc., New York

First Edition, 1970
Second Printing, 1971
This Printing, 1972

Library of Congress Catalog Card Number: 72-140207

SBN (cloth) 7178-0313-9; (paperback) 7178-0314-7

Printed in the United States of America

This book is dedicated to
the workers and peasants of Africa.

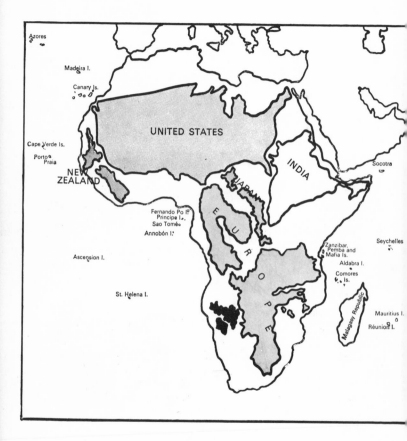

AREA OF AFRICA AND ITS ISLANDS:
c. 12,000,000 sq. miles

POPULATION:
c. 500 million

CONTENTS

INTRODUCTION

In Africa where so many different kinds of political, social and economic conditions exist it is not an easy task to generalise on political and socio-economic patterns. Remnants of communalism and feudalism still remain and in parts of the continent ways of life have changed very little from traditional times. In other areas a high level of industrialisation and urbanisation has been achieved. Yet in spite of Africa's socio-economic and political diversity it is possible to discern certain common political, social and economic conditions and problems. These derive from traditional past, common aspirations, and from shared experience under imperialism, colonialism and neocolonialism. There is no part of the continent which has not known oppression and exploitation, and no part which remains outside the processes of the African Revolution. Everywhere, the underlying unity of purpose of the peoples of Africa is becoming increasingly evident, and no African leader can survive who does not pay at least lip service to the African revolutionary objectives of total liberation, unification and socialism.

In this situation, the ground is well prepared for the next crucial phase of the Revolution, when the armed struggle which has now emerged must be intensified, expanded and effectively co-ordinated at strategic and tactical levels; and at the same time, a determined attack must be made on the entrenched position of the minority reactionary elements amongst our own peoples. For the dramatic exposure in recent years of the nature and extent of the class struggle in Africa, through the succession of reactionary military coups and the outbreak of civil wars, particularly in West and Central Africa, has demonstrated the unity between the interests of neocolonialism and the indigenous bourgeoisie.

At the core of the problem is the class struggle. For too long, social and political commentators have talked and written as though Africa lies outside the main stream of world historical development—a separate entity to which the social, economic and political patterns of the world do not apply. Myths such as "African socialism" and "pragmatic socialism", implying the existence of a brand or brands of socialism applicable to Africa alone, have been propagated; and much of our history has been written in terms of socio-anthropological and historical theories as though Africa had no history prior to the colonial period. One of these distortions has been the suggestion that the class structures which exist in other parts of the world do not exist in Africa.

Nothing is further from the truth. A fierce class struggle has been raging in Africa. The evidence is all around us. In essence it is, as in the rest of the world, a struggle between the oppressors and the oppressed.

The African Revolution is an integral part of the world socialist revolution, and just as the class struggle is basic to world revolutionary processes, so also is it fundamental to the struggle of the workers and peasants of Africa.

Class divisions in modern African society became blurred to some extent during the pre-independence period, when it seemed there was national unity and all classes joined forces to eject the colonial power. This led some to proclaim that there were no class divisions in Africa, and that the communalism and egalitarianism of traditional African society made any notion of a class struggle out of the question. But the exposure of this fallacy followed quickly after independence, when class cleavages which had been temporarily submerged in the struggle to win political freedom reappeared, often with increased intensity, particularly in those states where the newly independent government embarked on socialist policies.

For the African bourgeoisie, the class which thrived under colonialism, is the same class which is benefiting under the post-independence, neocolonial period. Its basic interest lies in preserving capitalist social and economic structures. It is therefore, in alliance with international monopoly finance capital.

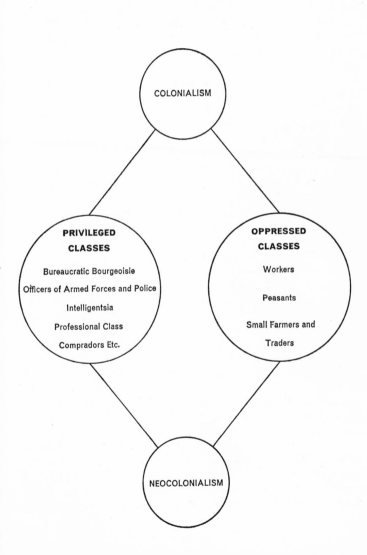

and neocolonialism, and in direct conflict with the African masses, whose aspirations can only be fulfilled through scientific socialism.

Although the African bourgeoisie is small numerically, and lacks the financial and political strength of its counterparts in the highly industrialised countries, it gives the illusion of being economically strong because of its close tie-up with foreign finance capital and business interests. Many members of the African bourgeoisie are employed by foreign firms and have, therefore, a direct financial stake in the continuance of the foreign economic exploitation of Africa. Others, notably in the civil service, trading and mining firms, the armed forces, the police and in the professions, are committed to capitalism because of their background, their western education, and their shared experience and enjoyment of positions of privilege. They are mesmerised by capitalist institutions and organisations. They ape the way of life of their old colonial masters, and are determined to preserve the status and power inherited from them.

Africa has in fact in its midst a hard core of bourgeoisie who are analogous to colonists and settlers in that they live in positions of privilege—a small, selfish, money-minded, reactionary minority among vast masses of exploited and oppressed people. Although apparently strong because of their support from neocolonialists and imperialists, they are extremely vulnerable. Their survival depends on foreign support. Once this vital link is broken, they become powerless to maintain their positions and privileges. They and the "hidden hand" of neocolonialism and imperialism which supports and abets reaction and exploitation now tremble before the rising tide of worker and peasant awareness of the class struggle in Africa.

1

ORIGINS OF CLASS IN AFRICA

Africa and its islands, with a land area of some twelve million square miles and a population estimated at about 500 million, could easily contain within it, and with room to spare, the whole of India, Europe, Japan, the British Isles, Scandinavia and New Zealand. The United States of America could easily be fitted into the Sahara Desert. Africa is geographically compact, and in terms of natural resources potentially the richest continent in the world.

In Africa, where economic development is uneven, a wide variety of highly sophisticated political systems were in existence over many centuries before the colonial period began. It is here, in the so-called developing world of Africa, and in Asia and Latin America, where the class struggle and the progress towards ending the exploitation of man by man have already entered into the stage of decisive revolutionary change.

The political maturity of the African masses may to some extent be traced to economic and social patterns of traditional times. Under communalism, for example, all land and means of production belonged to the community. There was people's ownership. Labour was the need and habit of all. When a certain piece of land was allocated to an individual for his personal use, he was not free to do as he liked with it since it still belonged to the community. Chiefs were strictly controlled by counsellors and were removable.

There have been five major types of production relationships known to man—communalism, slavery, feudalism, capitalism and socialism. With the establishment of the socialist state, man has embarked on the road to communism. It was when private

13

property relationships emerged, and as communalism gave way to slavery and feudalism, that the class struggle began.

In general, at the opening of the colonial period, the peoples of Africa were passing through the higher stage of communalism characterised by the disintegration of tribal democracy and the emergence of feudal relationships, hereditary tribal chieftaincies and monarchical systems. With the impact of imperialism and colonialism, communalist socio-economic patterns began to collapse as a result of the introduction of export crops such as cocoa and coffee. The economies of the colonies became interconnected with world capitalist markets. Capitalism, individualism, and tendencies to private ownership grew. Gradually, primitive communalism disintegrated and the collective spirit declined. There was an expansion of private farming and the method of small commodity production.

It was a relatively easy matter for white settlers to appropriate land which was not individually owned. For example, in Malawi, by 1892, more than sixteen per cent of the land had been alienated, and three quarters of it was under the direction of eleven big companies. When the land was seized by settlers, the African "owners" became in some cases tenants or lease-holders, but only on land considered not fertile enough for white farmers. The latter were usually issued with certificates of ownership of land by the British consul, acting on behalf of the British government; and any land not under any specific private ownership was declared "British crown land". Similar arrangements were made in other parts of colonial Africa.

Under colonialism, communal ownership of land was finally abolished and ownership of land imposed by law. Furthermore, through the system of "Indirect Rule", chiefs became tools, and in many cases paid agents, of the colonial administration.

With the seizure of the land, with all its natural resources—that is, the means of production, two sectors of the economy emerged—the European and the African, the former exploiting the latter. Subsistence agriculture was gradually destroyed and Africans were compelled to sell their labour power to the colonialists, who turned their profits into capital. It was in these circumstances that the race-class struggle also emerged as part of the class struggle.

With the growth of commodity production, mainly for export, single crop economies developed completely dependent on foreign capital. The colony became a sphere for investment and exploitation. Capitalism developed with colonialism. At the same time, the spread of private enterprise, together with the needs of th colonial administrative apparatus, resulted in the emergence of first a petty bourgeois class and then an urban bourgeois class of bureaucrats, reactionary intellectuals, traders, and others, who became increasingly part and parcel of the colonial economic and social structure.

To facilitate exploitation, colonialism hampered social and cultural progress in the colonies. Obsolete forms of social relations were restored and preserved. Capitalist methods of production, and capitalist social relationships were introduced. Friction between tribes was in some cases deliberately encouraged when it served to strengthen the hands of colonial administrators.

But certain economic developments, such as that of the extractive industry, plantations and capitalist farming, the building of ports, roads and railways was undertaken in the interests of capitalism. As a result, social changes occurred. Feudal and semi-feudal relationships were undermined with the emergence of an industrial and agricultural proletariat. At the same time there developed a national bourgeoisie and an intelligentsia.

In this colonialist situation, African workers regarded the colonialists, foreign firms and foreign planters, as the exploiters. Thus their class struggle became in the first instance anti-imperialist, and not directed against the indigenous bourgeoisie. It is this which has been responsible in some degree for the relatively slow awakening of the African worker and peasant to the existence of their true class enemy —the indigenous bourgeoisie.

At the end of the colonial period there was in most African states a highly developed state machine and a veneer of Parliamentary democracy concealing a coercive state run by an elite of bureaucrats with practically unlimited power. There was an intelligentsia, completely indoctrinated with western values; a virtually non-existent labour movement; a professional army and a police force with an officer corps largely trained in western military academies; and a chieftaincy used to administering at local level on behalf of the colonial government.

But on the credit side, a new grass roots political leadership emerged during the independence struggle. This was based on worker and peasant support, and committed not only to the winning of political freedom but to a complete transformation of society. This revolutionary leadership, although of necessity associated with the national bourgeoisie in the independence struggle was quite separate from it, and proceeded to break away after independence to pursue its class socialist objectives. This struggle still continues.

2

CLASS CONCEPT

Class struggle is a fundamental theme of recorded history. In every non-socialist society there are two main categories of class, the ruling class or classes, and the subject class or classes. The ruling class possesses the major instruments of economic production and distribution, and the means of establishing its political dominance, while the subject class serves the interests of the ruling class, and is politically, economically and socially dominated by it. There is conflict between the ruling class and the exploited class. The nature and cause of the conflict is influenced by the development of productive forces. That is, in any given class formation, whether it be feudalism, capitalism, or any other type of society, the institutions and ideas associated with it arise from the level of productive forces and the mode of production. The moment private ownership of the means of production appears, and capitalists start exploiting workers the capitalists become a bourgeois class, the exploited workers a working class. For in the final analysis, a class is nothing more than the sum total of individuals bound together by certain interests which as a class they try to preserve and protect.

Every form of political power, whether parliamentary, multi-party, one-party or open military dictatorship, reflects the interest of a certain class or classes in society. In socialist states the government represents workers and peasants. In capitalist states, the government represents the exploiting class, The state then, is the expression of the domination of one class over other classes.

Similarly, political parties represent the existence of different

17

classes. It might be assumed from this that a single party state denotes classlessness. But this is not necessarily the case. It only applies if the state represents political power held by the people. In many states, where two or more political parties exist, and where there are sharp class cleavages, there is to all intents and purposes government by a single party. In the case of the United States of America, for example, Republican and Democratic Parties may be said to be in fact a single party in

CLASS STRUGGLE

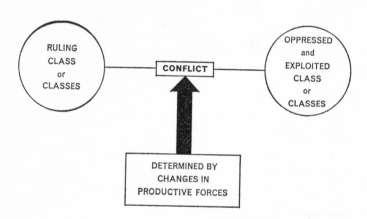

that they represent a single class, the propertied class. In Britain, there is in practice little difference between the Conservative Party and the Labour Party. The Labour Party founded to promote the interests of the working class has in fact developed into a bourgeois oriented party. Both the Conservative Party and the Labour Party are therefore expressions of the bourgeoisie and reflect its ideology.

18

Inequality can only be ended by the abolition of classes. The division between those who plan, organise and manage, and those who actually perform the manual labour, continually re-creates the class system. The individual usually finds it very difficult, if not impossible, to break out of the sphere of life into which he is born; and even where there is "equality of opportunity", the underlying assumption of inequality remains, where the purpose of "opportunity" is to aspire to a higher level in a stratified society.

A ruling class is cohesive and conscious of itself as a class. It has objective interests, is aware of its position and the threat posed to its continued dominance by the rising tide of working class revolt. In Africa, the ruling classes account for approximately only one per cent of the population. Some 80–90 per cent of the population consists of peasants and agricultural labourers. Urban and industrial workers represent about five per cent. Yet because of the presence of foreigners and foreign interests, class struggle in African society has been blurred. Conflict between the African peoples and the interests of neo-colonialism, colonialism, imperialism and settler regimes, has concealed all other contradictory forces. This explains to some extent why class or vanguard parties have been so long emerging in Africa.

Broadly, the existing class pattern of African society may be shown as follows:

Classes	Divisions Within Classes	Elites
PEASANTS		
PROLETARIAT (wage-earning)	– rural, labourers, etc. – industrial (mainly employed in major industries, mining, transport, etc.)	

continued overleaf

Classes	Divisions Within Classes	Elites
PETTY BOURGEOISIE (a) Farmers (rural petty bourgeoisie, owning land and employing labour) (b) Urban petty bourgeoisie (small traders, merchants craftsmen, etc.)	– social status determined by size of land-holding, and amount of labour employed – status according to size of business and property	
BOURGEOISIE (including national bourgeoisie, and representing capitalism.) – traders, tradesmen, – top civil servants – compradors (managers or senior employees of foreign enterprises) – entrepreneurs – professional and managerial "class", etc.	– upper – middle	– intellectuals – top bureaucrats – officer "class" in armed forces – professionals (top lawyers, doctors, etc) – technocrats.
TRADITIONAL RULERS (authority based mainly on tradition, custom, etc., and *not* land ownership)	– clan heads – chiefs – paramount chiefs – emirs, etc.	

The uneven economic development of Africa has made for a variety of class patterns with wide differences existing between the areas of white settler minority governments, the few remaining colonial enclaves, and independent Africa.

For example, in Rhodesia, four million Africans are crowded into less than half the land acreage of the country. In other words, more than half the land is in the hands of some 500,000 white settlers. This state of affairs has resulted in an enormous social and political gulf between the rich, white estate owners and the impoverished politically-impotent African peasants and workers. Here, as in all settler areas, class is a race issue first and foremost—the "haves" are white, the "have-nots" are black—and all the usual arguments—the myth of racial inferiority, the need for government by the most able, and so on—are used to justify perpetuation of the enforced, racialist, settler arrangement.

Again, in francophone Africa, social patterns have resulted in the emergence of class divisions peculiar to this particular colonised area. There were the "citoyens", the French "colons" or citizens. There were the "assimilés", the coloured mulattoes and the black intelligentsia, or those Africans who worked their way to this class through the Army or the bureaucracy. Then came the "sujets", the workers and peasants. An "assimilé" could become a "citoyen", but a "sujet" could not, unless he first worked his way into the "assimilé" class. This type of social system operated in all the French colonies. Analogous arrangements still exist in the few remaining Spanish and Portuguese territories in Africa.

The assimilation policy meant that any colonial "subject" could be naturalised as a full French citizen. In practice, however, even those who reached a high enough level of education usually did not attempt to avail themselves of this so-called privilege, largely because, except in the Four Communes, French citizenship was incompatible with the retention of one's personal status—that is, the right to live by African customary law as opposed to the French *code civil*. There was a certain logic in this from a strictly assimilationist point of view: if one was going to be a Frenchman in the political sense, then one should behave like one socially, and accept such institutions as monogamy and French inheritance laws. But its effect underlined the failure of assimilation, for on these terms, assimilation was not a saleable commodity; and so, outside the Four Communes, "citizen" remained virtually synonymous with "white Frenchman".

While the nature of the economic relationship between the colony and its metropolitan master determined the nature of the class conflict in a particular area, other factors included the ideas and customs of the invading power, although these were attributable ultimately to changes in the structure of productive relations.

In areas colonised by the British, a certain amount of urbanisation made for the emergence of bourgeois and petty bourgeois elites which developed their own class characteristic attitudes and organisations. To obtain a "white collar" job became the ambition of every African aspiring to improve his prospects and social status. Manual work, particularly agricultural work, was considered beneath the dignity of anyone who had acquired even the most rudimentary degree of education.

In pre-colonial Africa, under conditions of communalism, slavery and feudalism there were embryonic class cleavages. But it was not until the era of colonial conquest that a Europeanised class structure began to develop with clearly identifiable classes of proletariat and bourgeoisie. This development has always been played down by reactionary observers, most of whom have maintained that African societies are homogeneous and without class divisions. They have even endeavoured to retain this view in the face of glaring evidence of class struggle shown in the post-independence period, when bourgeois elements have joined openly with neocolonialists, colonialists and imperialists in vain attempts to keep the African masses in permanent subjection.

3

CLASS CHARACTERISTICS AND IDEOLOGIES

There is a close connection between socio-political development, the struggle between social classes and the history of ideologies. In general, intellectual movements closely reflect the trends of economic developments. In communal society, where there are virtually no class divisions, man's productive activities exert a direct influence on his outlook and aesthetic tastes. But in a class society, the direct influence of productive activities on outlook and culture is less discernible. Account must be taken of the psychology of conflicting classes.

Certain social habits, dress, institutions and organisations are associated with different classes. It is possible to place a person in a particular class simply by observing his general appearance, his dress and the way he behaves. Similarly, each class has its own characteristic institutions and organisations. For example, co-operatives and trade unions are organisations of the working class. Professional associations, chambers of commerce, stock exchanges, rotary clubs, masonic societies, and so on, are middle class, bourgeois institutions.

Ideologies reflect class interests and class consciousness. Liberalism, individualism, elitism, and bourgeois "democracy"—which is an illusion—are examples of bourgeois ideology. Fascism, imperialism, colonialism, and neocolonialism are also expressions of bourgeois thinking and of bourgeois political and economic aspirations. On the other hand, socialism and communism are ideologies of the working class, and reflect its aspirations and politico-economic institutions and organisations.

The bourgeois conception of freedom as the absence of restraint, of laissez-faire, free enterprise, and of "every man for himself", is a typical expression of bourgeois ideology. The basic thesis is that the purpose of government is to protect private property and the private ownership of the means of production and distribution. Freedom is confined to the political sphere, and has no relevance to economic matters. Capitalism, which knows no law beyond its own interest, is equated

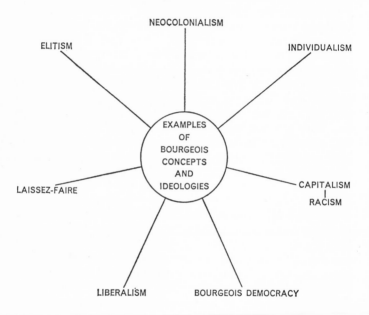

with economic freedom. Inseparable from this conception of freedom is the view that the presence or absence of wealth denotes the presence or absence of ability.

Coupled with the bourgeois conception of freedom is the bourgeois worship of "law and order" regardless of who made the law, or of whether it serves the interests of the people, a class or of a narrow elite.

In recent years, in the face of growing revolutionary violence throughout the world, new misleading bourgeois terminology has emerged which expresses the reactionary back-lash. Typical examples are the myths of the "silent majority" or the "average" or "ordinary citizen", both of which are said to be anti-revolutionary and in favour of maintaining the status quo. In fact, in any capitalist society, the working class forms the majority and this class is far from silent, and is vocal in its demand for a radical transformation of society.

In Africa, the African bourgeoisie, anxious to emulate European middle class attitudes and ideologies, have in many cases confused class with race. They find it difficult to differentiate between European classes since they are not familiar with the subtle differences in speech, manners, dress and so on—differences which would instantly betray their class origin to their own fellow countrymen. Members of the European working class live as bourgeoisie in the colonies. They own cars, have servants, their women do not enter the kitchen, and their class origin is only apparent to their own people. After independence, the indigenous bourgeoisie, in aspiring to ruling class status, copy the way of life of the ex-ruling class—the Europeans. They are, in reality, imitating a race and not a class.

The African bourgeoisie, therefore, tends to live the kind of life lived by the old colonial ruling class, which is not necessarily the way of life of the European bourgeoisie. It is rather the way of life of a racial group in a colonial situation. In this sense, the African bourgeoisie perpetuates the master-servant relationships of the colonial period.

Although the African bourgeoisie for the most part slavishly accepts the ideologies of its counterparts in the capitalist world, there are certain ideologies which have developed specifically within the African context, and which have become characteristic expressions of African bourgeois mentality. Perhaps the most typical is the bogus conception of "negritude". This pseudo-intellectual theory serves as a bridge between the African foreign-dominated middle class and the French cultural establishment. It is irrational, racist and non-revolutionary. It reflects the confused state of mind of some of the colonised

French African intellectuals, and is totally divorced from the reality of the African Personality.

The term "African socialism" is similarly meaningless and irrelevant. It implies the existence of a form of socialism peculiar to Africa and derived from communal and egalitarian aspects of traditional African society. The myth of African socialism is used to deny the class struggle, and to obscure genuine socialist commitment. It is employed by those African leaders who are compelled—in the climate of the African Revolution—to proclaim socialist policies, but who are at the same time deeply committed to international capitalism, and who do not intend to promote genuine socialist economic development.

While there is no hard and fast dogma for socialist revolution, and specific circumstances at a definite historical period will determine the precise form it will take, there can be no compromise over socialist goals. The principles of scientific socialism are universal and abiding, and involve the genuine socialisation of productive and distributive processes. Those who for political reasons pay lip service to socialism, while aiding and abetting imperialism and neocolonialism, serve bourgeois class interests. Workers and peasants may be misled for a time, but as class consciousness develops the bogus socialists are exposed, and genuine socialist revolution is made possible.

4

CLASS AND RACE

Each historical situation develops its own dynamics. The close links between class and race developed in Africa alongside capitalist exploitation. Slavery, the master-servant relationship, and cheap labour were basic to it. The classic example is South Africa, where Africans experience a double exploitation—both on the ground of colour and of class. Similar conditions exist in the U.S.A., the Caribbean, in Latin America, and in other parts of the world where the nature of the development of productive forces has resulted in a racist class structure. In these areas, even shades of colour count—the degree of blackness being a yardstick by which social status is measured.

While a racist social structure is not inherent in the colonial situation, it is inseparable from capitalist economic development. For race is inextricably linked with class exploitation; in a racist-capitalist power structure, capitalist exploitation and race oppression are complementary; the removal of one ensures the removal of the other.

In the modern world, the race struggle has become part of the class struggle. In other words, wherever there is a race problem it has become linked with the class struggle.

The effects of industrialisation in Africa as elsewhere, has been to foster the growth of the bourgeoisie, and at the same time the growth of a politically-conscious proletariat. The acquisition of property and political power on the part of the bourgeoisie, and the growing socialist and African nationalist aspirations of the working class, both strike at the root of the racist class structure, though each is aiming at different objectives. The bourgeoisie supports capitalist development while the proletariat—the oppressed class—is striving towards socialism.

In South Africa, where the basis of ethnic relationships is class and colour, the bourgeoisie comprises about one-fifth of the population. The British and the Boers, having joined forces

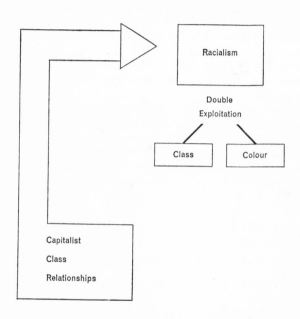

to maintain their positions of privilege, have split up the remaining four-fifths of the population into "Blacks", "Coloureds" and "Indians". The Coloureds and Indians are minority groups which act as buffers to protect the minority Whites against the increasingly militant and revolutionary Black majority. In the other settler areas of Africa, a similar class-race struggle is being waged.

A non-racial society can only be achieved by socialist revolutionary action of the masses. It will never come as a gift from the minority ruling class. For it is impossible to separate race relations from the capitalist class relationships in which they have their roots.

South Africa again provides a typical example. In the early years of Dutch settlement, the distinction was made not between Black and White, but between Christian and Heathen. It was only with capitalist economic penetration that the master-servant relationship emerged, and with it, racism, colour prejudice and apartheid. The latter is the most intolerable and iniquitous of policies and race-class "systems" ever to emerge from White, capitalist, bourgeois society. Eighty per cent of the population of South Africa is non-white and has no vote or political rights.

Slavery and the master-servant relationship were therefore the cause, rather than the result of, racism. The position was crystallized and reinforced with the discovery of gold and diamonds in South Africa, and the employment of cheap African labour in the mines. As time passed, and it was thought necessary to justify the exploitation and oppression of African workers, the myth of racial inferiority was developed and spread.

In the era of neocolonialism, "under-development" is still attributed not to exploitation but to inferiority, and racial undertones remain closely interwoven with the class struggle.

It is only the ending of capitalism, colonialism, imperialism and neocolonialism and the attainment of world communism that can provide the conditions under which the race question can finally be abolished and eliminated.

5

ELITISM

Elitism is an ideology of the bourgeoisie. It arose during the second half of the nineteenth century largely as a result of the work of two Italian sociologists, Vilfredo Pareto (1848–1923) and Gaetano Mosca (1858–1941). They wrote at a time when the middle class, which had recently gained political power from the aristocracy, felt in its turn threatened from below by a rapidly growing working class imbued with Marxist ideology. Pareto and Mosca aimed to refute Marx and to deny the possibility of socialist revolution leading to a classless society. Unlike Marx, they maintained that political skill determined who ruled, and that society would always be governed by some kind of elite, or a combination of elites.

In essence, elitists assert that in practice the minority always exercises effective power, and that the dominant minority can never be controlled by the majority, no matter what so-called democratic institutions are employed. The cohesiveness of elites constitute their main strength. They are small in relation to the nation as a whole, but they are strong out of proportion to their size.

Elitism is an ideology tailor-made to fit capitalism and bourgeois de facto domination in the capitalist society. Furthermore, it intensifies racism, since it can be used to subscribe to the myth of racial superiority and inferiority.

In recent times, there has been a great revival of interest in the study of elites, and many new elitist theories have been disseminated. It is significant that this development coincides historically with a tremendous upsurge of socialist revolutionary activity in the world. Bourgeois theorists, seeking to justify the continuance of capitalism, have found it necessary to fall back on elitism. They cannot by any rational argument justify the harsh irrationality of capitalism. So they try to show that there will always be a ruling elite, and that government is always in the hands of those most fitted to govern. In maintaining this, they evade the reality of the economic class structure and class struggle in capitalist society.

Among the basic tenets of elitism is the theory that power breeds power, and that apathy, submissiveness and deference are qualities of the masses in politics. Democracy has been defined as competition between oligarchies. It has become fashionable to talk of top decision-makers, and to discuss which group or groups really wield power in a state. Is there a concentration or a diffusion of power? How are political decisions made? Are they made by a ruling elite? Do the masses exercise any measure of indirect power? Or are decisions made by diverse elite groupings? Is it true that: "Governments do not govern, but merely control the machinery of government, being themselves controlled by the hidden hand"?

Pluralists assert that power is not held by a single elite, but by a mixture of many. Power is regarded as cumulative—wealth, social status, and political power being interwoven. Connected with this view is the idea of "elite consensus"—that is, the involvement in policy formation of only the most important elite groupings.

It was one of the declared aims of the early elitists to demolish the myths of "democracy". They set out to show that in so-called democracies, the people, or a majority of the people do not in fact rule, but that government is carried out by a narrow elite. They went even further and asserted that participation in government was not a necessary feature of democracy, and not in itself an important ideal.

There can be no class within a class, but there are elites within a class. Elites arise from the development and formation of a class. In Europe, the broad class pattern is as follows:

Traditional aristocracy   – based on land and titles

| Middle class | – based on money, and divided into upper, middle and lower |
| Working class | – based on agriculture and industry, and divided into upper and lower. |

Among the middle class—the new aristocracy—are plutocrats, managers, intellectuals, bureaucrats, technocrats, and so on, each of which may be said to constitute an elite. With the rapid development of technology, and increasing specialisation, the strata of technocrats—an elite within the middle class—is becoming increasingly influential in decision-making. Some elitists assert that a meritocracy—government by the "expert"—is now a reality.

European-style elites may be discerned among the African bourgeoisie. Under colonialism, the African elites were chiefs in the colonial legislative councils and in the colonial administrative services; lawyers and doctors; judges and magistrates; top civil servants; senior army and police officers. After independence, the old elites remained virtually intact, and acquired greater strength. The position of members of Parliament and National Assemblies, cabinet ministers, top civil servants, senior army and police officers, and so on, were enhanced. They were no longer subordinate to colonial authority. Members of the professions, for example, teachers, lawyers and doctors, benefited by the Africanisation policies of the newly-independent government.

It was in the post-independence period that there emerged what may be termed the "party *nouveaux riches*", an elite which developed from among the ranks of the Party which successfully won political freedom from the colonial power. After independence, conflict develops within the Party between Right and Left wing elements. The Rightists become the Party *nouveaux riches*. They proceed to make their fortunes once independence has been achieved, and the Party has become the governing Party. They exploit their new positions of power and indulge in nepotism and corruption, thereby discrediting the

Party and helping to pave the way for reactionary coups d'état.

Similarly, after independence, and with the implementation of economic Development Plans, and the encouragement in some cases of indigenous business enterprise, local budding capitalists to some extent acquired new opportunities to extend their interests. But in general, African capitalists are still the junior partners of imperialism. They receive the crumbs of investment profits, commercial agencies, commissions, and directorships of foreign-owned firms. In these, and in many other ways, they are drawn into the web of neocolonialism.

As a result of colonialism and neocolonialism, there has been comparatively little development of an African business elite. In addition, the fact that many newly-independent governments tend to concentrate on the public rather than on the private sector of the economy, has led to the relatively small size of the African capitalist class. The African business man is, in general, not so much interested in developing industry as in seeking to enrich himself by speculation, black marketeering, corruption and the receipt of commissions from contracts, and by various financial manipulations connected with the receipt of so-called "aid". The African capitalist thus becomes the class ally of the bourgeoisie of the capitalist world. He is a pawn in the immense network of international monopoly finance capital.

In this way, he is closely connected with, for example, the giant corporations of monopoly capitalism. It has been asserted that in the U.S.A. the "finpols", that is, the financial politicians, exercise decisive power and are responsible for major decision-making. This is done through "finpolities"—huge corporations such as the Ford Motor Company, Du Pont and General Motors—to mention only a few. In 1953 there were more than 27,000 millionaires in the U.S.A., and the concentration of wealth in a few hands is intensifying. It is estimated that 1.6 per cent of the population owns at least 32 per cent of all assets, and nearly all investment assets; and 50 per cent of the population owns practically nothing. It cannot be said that power in the U.S.A. is in the hands of the most

33

qualified, since most of the wealth is inherited, and its possession, therefore, does not necessarily denote merit.

Yet it has been held by some elitists that development of industrial societies can be shown as a movement from a class system to a system of elites based on merit and achievement. Such a theory falls to the ground in the light of clear evidence of the sharpening of class struggle throughout the capitalist world.

Among elitists, opinions differ as to how far elites can be said to be cohesive, conscious, and conspiratorial. Obviously it is impossible to measure precisely the influence and decision-making power, and the degree of cohesiveness of any particular elite or group of elites.

Among the political elite in the developing countries are nationalist leaders, bureaucrats and intelligentsia. Of the members of the Ghana House of Assembly after the 1954 election, 29 per cent were school teachers and 17 per cent were members of the liberal professions. Among the Legislative Assembly members of the eight territories of the former French West Africa, after the 1957 elections, 22 per cent were teachers, 27 per cent were government officials, and 20 per cent were members of the professions.

The middle class in developing countries was in the main created by the educational and administrative systems introduced under colonialism. The predominance of the intelligentsia in the middle class is due in the main to the deliberate policy of the colonial power in fostering the growth of an intelligentsia geared to western ideologies which it needed for the successful functioning of the colonial administration. At the same time the colonial power curbed opportunities for the formation of an indigenous business class.

Elite associations, such as bar associations, medical societies, oddfellows, freemasonry, rotary clubs, etc., emerge with the development of elites. These associations assist class formation by institutionalising social differences. The existence of class feeling is shown in the desire to join associations and clubs which are thought to enhance social status.

Elitism is basic to the thinking of those who accept class

stratification. It is an ingredient of capitalism, and is further intensified by racism, which in its turn is a result of the growth of capitalism and imperialism. The inherent elitism of the ruling classes makes them contemptuous of the masses. Elitism is an enemy of socialism and of the working class.

6

INTELLIGENTSIA AND INTELLECTUALS

Under colonialism, an intelligentsia educated in western ideology emerged and provided a link between the colonial power and the masses. It was drawn for the most part from the families of chiefs and from the "moneyed" sections of the population. The growth of the intelligentsia was limited to the minimum needed for the functioning of the colonial administration. It became socially alienated, an elite susceptible both to Left and Right opportunism.

In Africa, as in Europe and elsewhere, education largely determines class. As literacy increases, tribal and ethnic allegiances weaken, and class divisions sharpen. There is what may be described as an *esprit de corps*, particularly among those who have travelled abroad for their education. They become alienated from tribal and village roots, and in general, their aims are political power, social position, and professional status. Even today, when many independent states have built excellent schools, colleges and universities, thousands of Africans prefer to study abroad. There are at present, some 10,000 African students in France, 10,000 in Britain, and 2,000 in the U.S.A.

In areas of Africa which were once ruled by the British, English type public schools were introduced during the colonial period. In Ghana, Adisadel, Mfantsipim and Achimota are typical examples. In these schools, and in similar schools built throughout British colonies in Africa, curriculum, discipline and sports were as close imitations as possible of those operating in English public schools. The object was to train up a western-oriented political elite committed to the attitudes and ideologies of capitalism and bourgeois society.

In Britain, the English class system is largely based on education. The three per cent products of English public schools are still considered by many to be the country's "natural rulers"—that is, those best qualified to rule both both by birth and education. For in Britain, the educational structure is inseparable from the political and social framework. While only six per cent of the population attends public schools, and only five per cent go to university, the public schools provide 60 per cent of the nation's company directors, 70 per cent of Conservative members of Parliament, and 50 per cent of those appointed to Royal Commissions and public inquiries. In other words, the small minority of products of exclusive educational establishments, occupy the large majority of top positions in the economic and political life of the country. This irrational and outdated "system" still continues to operate in spite of apparent efforts to widen and popularise educational opportunities. It has not yet been seriously challenged by the growing importance of the experts or technocrats, most of them educated in grammar and comprehensive schools. Nor has it shown any significant weakening in the face of growing political pressure from below. In fact, if they could afford it, the majority of working-class parents would send their children to public schools because of the unique opportunities they provide for entry into top positions in society.

The products of English public schools have their counterparts in the British ex-colonial territories. These are the bourgeois establishment figures who try to be more British than the British, and who imitate the dress, manners and even the voices of the British public school and Oxbridge elite.

The colonialists' aim in fostering the growth of an African intelligentsia is "to form local cadres called upon to become our assistants in all fields, and to ensure the development of a carefully selected elite". This, to them, is a political and economic necessity. And how do they do it? "We pick our pupils primarily from among the children of chiefs and aristocrats. . . . The prestige due to origin should be backed up by respect which possession of knowledge evokes."

In 1953, before Ghana's independence, out of a total of 208 students at the University college, 12 per cent of the families of students had an income of over £600 a year; 38 per cent between £250 and £600; and 50 per cent about £250. The significance of these figures is seen when it is realised that it was only in 1962, after vigorous efforts in the economic field, that it was possible to get the average annual income per head of the population up to approximately £94.

Unlike the British and the French, the Belgians were against allowing the growth of an intelligentsia. "No elite, no trouble" appeared to be their motto. The results of such a policy were clearly seen in the Congo, for example, in 1960 when there was scarcely a qualified Congolese in the country to run the newly-independent state, to officer the army and police, or to fill the many administrative and technical posts left by the departing colonialists.

The intelligentsia always leads the nationalist movement in its early stages. It aspires to replace the colonial power, but not to bring about a radical transformation of society. The object is to control the "system" rather than to change it, since the intelligentsia tends as a whole to be bourgeois-minded and against revolutionary socialist transformation.

The cohesiveness of the intelligentsia before independence disappears once independence is achieved. It divides roughly into three main groups. First, there are those who support the new privileged indigenous class—the bureaucratic, political and business bourgeoisie who are the open allies of imperialism and neocolonialism. These members of the intelligentsia produce the ideologists of anti-socialism and anti-communism and of capitalist political and economic values and concepts.

Secondly, there are those who advocate a "non-capitalist road" of economic development, a "mixed economy", for the less industrialised areas of the world, as a phase in the progress towards socialism. This concept, if misunderstood and misapplied, can probably be more dangerous to the socialist revolutionary cause in Africa than the former open pro-capitalism, since it may seem to promote socialism, whereas in fact it may retard the process. History has proved, and is still proving, that a non-capitalist road, unless it is treated as a very temporary phase in the progress towards socialism, positively hinders its growth. By allowing capitalism and private enterprise to exist in a state committed to socialism, the seeds of a reactionary seizure of power may be sown. The private sector of the economy continually tries to expand beyond the limits within which it is confined, and works ceaselessly to curb and undermine the socialist policies of the socialist-oriented government. Eventually, more often than not, if all else fails, it succeeds, with the help of neocolonialists, in organising a reactionary coup d'état to oust the socialist-oriented government.

The third section of the intelligentsia to emerge after independence consists of the revolutionary intellectuals—those who provide the impetus and leadership of the worker-peasant struggle for all-out socialism. It is from among this section that the genuine intellectuals of the African Revolution are to be found. Very often they are minority products of colonial educational establishments who reacted strongly against its brainwashing processes and who became genuine socialist and African nationalist revolutionaries. It is the task of this third section of the intelligentsia to enunciate and promulgate African revolutionary socialist objectives, and to expose and refute the deluge of capitalist propaganda and bogus concepts and theories poured out by the imperialist, neocolonialist and indigenous, reactionary mass communications media.

Under conditions of capitalism and neocolonialism, the majority of students, teachers, university staff and others coming under the broad category of "intellectuals", are an elite within the bourgeoisie, and can become a revolutionary or a counter-revolutionary force for political action. Before independence, many of them become leaders of the nationalist revolution. After independence, they tend to split up. Those who helped in the nationalist revolutionary struggle take part in the government, and are oriented either to the Party *nouveaux riches*, or to the socialist revolutionaries. The others join the political opposition, or become apolitical, or advocate middle of the road policies. Some become dishonest intellectuals. For they see the irrationality of capitalism but enjoy its benefits and way of life; and for their own selfish reasons are prepared to prostitute themselves and become agents and supporters of privilege and reaction.

In general, intellectuals with working-class origins tend to be more radical than those from the privileged sectors of society. But intellectuals are probably the least cohesive or homogeneous of elites. Most of the intellectuals in the U.S.A., Britain and in Western Europe belong to the Right. Similarly, the aspirations of the majority of Africa's intellectuals are characteristic of the middle class. They seek power, prestige, wealth and social position for themselves and their families. Many of those from working-class families aspire to middle-class status, shrinking from manual work and becoming completely alienated from their class and social origins.

Where socialist revolutionary intellectuals have become part of genuinely progressive administrations in Africa, it has usually been through the adoption of Marxism as a political creed, and the formation of Communist parties or similar organisations which bring them into constant close contact with workers and peasants.

Intelligentsia and intellectuals, if they are to play a part in the African Revolution, must become conscious of the class struggle in Africa, and align themselves with the oppressed masses. This involves the difficult, but not impossible, task of cutting themselves free from bourgeois attitudes and ideologies imbibed as a result of colonialist education and propaganda.

The ideology of the African Revolution links the class struggle of African workers and peasants with world socialist revolutionary movements and with international socialism. It emerged during the national liberation struggle, and it continues to mature in the fight to complete the liberation of the continent, to achieve political unification, and to effect a socialist transformation of African society. It is unique. It has developed within the concrete situation of the African Revolution, is a product of the African Personality, and at the same time is based on the principles of scientific socialism.

7

REACTIONARY CLIQUES AMONG ARMED FORCES AND POLICE

The majority of Africa's armed forces and police came into existence as part of the colonial coercive apparatus. Few of their members joined national liberation struggles. For the most part, they were employed to perform police operations against it. In the colonial period, most of the officers were European. At independence, when Africanisation policies were put into operation, many Africans who were not really qualified to become officers received commissions because of the lack of suitable candidates. A large number were men who had held educational positions in the army, and were drawn from among the educated petty bourgeoisie. These and other older officers at present serving in Africa's armies were trained by colonialists or in military colleges of the West, and are therefore oriented towards Western norms and ideals. They may be said to form, because of their rank, part of the bureaucratic bourgeoisie, with a stake in the capitalist path of development.

Some of the younger officers, probably in their schooldays took part in the liberation struggle, and are therefore accessible to socialist revolutionary ideology. But although some of them have become supporters of the African Revolution, the majority of higher officers have succumbed to the same bourgeois indoctrination as their older fellow officers. They are closely linked socially, and in background and aspirations, with the bureaucratic bourgeoisie and with the reactionary officer elites in other countries.

In many cases, the officer class and the civil servants have shared similar educational experience in elite schools and colleges in Africa and overseas. They have developed similar outlooks and interests. They tend to distrust change, and to worship the organisations and institutions of capitalist bourgeois society. Even the younger generation of officers and bureaucrats who share power in many African states as a result of military coups, are steeped in attitudes and concepts which reflect the socio-political climate of the colonial period.

When neocolonialist coups take place, members of the armed forces, the police and the bureaucracy work together. This is not to say that they necessarily sit down together and plot coups, though this has sometimes been the case. But they have common interests and each needs the other. Bureaucrats alone cannot overthrow a government; and the military and police have not the expertise to administer a country. Therefore they combine, and bring about a state of affairs strikingly similar to that which operated in colonial times, when the colonial government depended on the civil service, on the army and police, and on the support of traditional rulers.

In almost every case where a coup has taken place there has been no mass participation. Workers and peasants are betrayed and coerced, and the clock put back to the conditions of colonialism. The power of reactionary traditional rulers is reinstated. The heavy reliance on the police in neocolonialist states is another reminder of the colonial period. Police officers, unlike army officers, are by the very nature of their work, in closer touch with the people. At the time of a coup, they are in a position to know exactly which elements to arrest, and where they should be confined. They know how to organise and to control riots and demonstrations. In many cases, police officers have themselves been involved in corruption. They are familiar with all aspects of crime, and do not shrink from any methods to obtain their ends. Like their counterparts in the armed forces, they have close links with the bureaucratic bourgeoisie, and share common interests.

The rank and file of army and police are from the peasantry. A large number are illiterate. They have been taught to obey orders without question, and have become tools of bourgeois capitalist interests. They are thus alienated from the peasant-worker struggle to which through their class origins they really belong. While to obey orders without question is a fundamental requirement of the ordinary soldier in most professional armies, it becomes extremely dangerous when those in a position to give orders serve the interests of only a small, privileged section of society. It means that the rank and file soldier or policeman can be used to bring about, and to maintain, reactionary regimes. In this, the ordinary soldier who is after all only a worker or peasant in uniform, is acting against the interests of his own class.

The solution to the problem lies in the politicising of army and police. Both must be firmly under the control of the socialist revolutionary Party, and commissions entrusted only to those who are fully committed to revolutionary socialist principles. At the same time, the discipline of the ordinary soldier and policeman must be based on understanding, and not on submissiveness and blind obedience. The mercenary aspect of military and police service should be ended, and a citizens' army and peoples' militia created. Workers, peasants, soldiers and policemen must work together. They belong to the same class and aspire to the same socialist revolution.

Compared with other class organisations, the army and police are more disciplined, mobile and technically equipped. Most important, they are armed, and provide therefore, a ready striking force. The use made of them depends on the ascendancy of this or that political trend within society, and the pressures, both internal and external, brought to bear on those in positions of command.

When the army intervenes in politics it does so as part of the class forces in society. Coups d'état are expressions of the class struggle and the struggle between imperialism and socialist revolution. The army, after it has seized power, gives its weight to one or other side. In this respect, the army is not merely an instrument in the struggle, but becomes itself part of the class struggle, thus tearing down the artificial wall separating it from the socio-economic and political transformations in society. The theory of the "neutrality" of the armed forces, consistently propagated by the exploiting classes, is thereby proved to be false.

The army when it intervenes in the political life of a country represents the dominant class interest of the small minority of those who organise and actually carry out the intervention. Presented with a *fait accompli*, the large majority of officers and men acquiesce. In Africa, although there have been a few coups which may be said to have paved the way for less reactionary regimes, by far the majority of them have been engineered by bourgeois-oriented officers who have had close links with the bureaucratic bourgeoisie, and with neocolonialists. Their joint aim is to protect capitalism and to frustrate the purposes of the African Socialist Revolution.

In some areas of Africa where army intervention has been proclaimed as revolutionary socialist, it has in fact been merely nationalist. The proclaimed aim is to end foreign exploitation and to improve the conditions of the people. Foreign firms are in some cases "nationalised", and foreign bases are closed down. But the conditions of the ordinary people remain practically the same as before the intervention. In place of foreign exploitation there is exploitation by the indigenous bourgeoisie. In no time, puppet regimes are installed. The country is in the grip of neocolonialism, and the bourgeoisie, either represented by stooge politicians or by bourgeois-minded army and police officers, is further entrenched. It is only when power is seized by workers and peasants that genuine socialist revolution can be achieved.

Immense sums of money have been spent on the upkeep of Africa's armies. The Congolese army, for example, received one-sixth of the state's revenue during the first four and a half years after independence; that is, it received some 25 billion out of 150 billion Congolese francs. In provisions of revenue budgets for 1967–68 in francophone Africa, eight out of fifteen states had provided the army with between 15 and 25 per cent of their resources. Mali, Guinea, Chad and Cameroun were prepared to devote up to one-quarter of their budgets for military purposes.

In general, officers' salaries are kept near to expatriate

level, and therefore vast differences in personal status and power exist between officers and men. The gap is much wider than between officers and men in Europe, the U.S.A., and elsewhere. In Africa, the differential between the pay of a lieutenant colonel and a recruit is ten or fifteen times greater than in Europe and America. The artificially high social status of the African officer class has the effect of heightening the already overbearing arrogant attitude which so many of them possess. To some extent, even the rank and file of army and police consider themselves to be a kind of elite. They usually earn more than clerks and other similar white collar workers. The developing practice of appointing army officers to high diplomatic posts when they are no longer required in the army is also an indication of the inflated position they occupy in African society.

There is little justification for the enormous sums of money spent on the armies of Africa. Africa is not threatened territorially by any outside power. The border disputes which exist between certain African states, most of them legacies from the colonial period, are all capable of peaceful solution. The struggles to end the remnants of colonialism and settler domination are not being fought by professional armies but by guerilla forces. If only a fraction of the amount spent by most states on their professional forces was diverted to support and equip African freedom fighters, the result would be a tremendous quickening of the pace of the African Revolution. The only valid reason which could justify the creation of large conventional armed forces is the vital necessity to achieve the objectives of the African Revolution, that is, the political unification of Africa, for which a unified All-African High Command is an essential prerequisite.

When faced with a political crisis the army tends to split along the same lines as the political community. In other words, it tends to divide along lines of class and sometimes tribe. The officer strata tends to be on the whole conservative, if not downright reactionary. It will usually side with the old established order. Historically, professional armies of the capitalist world have a tradition of suppression of socialist and

45

revolutionary movements. They are the instruments of the ruling class or classes for maintaining bourgeois power.

Compared with the armies of Europe, Asia and North and South America, the armies of Africa are relatively small in size. Only three countries south of the Sahara—Sudan, Ethiopia and Congo Kinshasa—have armies exceeding 10,000 men. Fourteen African states have armies of less than 2,000 men. Yet because of the small population of many of the independent states, and their non-viable economies, the maintaining of these armies places an intolerable burden on the state. Furthermore, because the armies of Africa are for the most part under the control of officers who have interests in common with the bureaucratic bourgeoisie and with neocolonialism, they have been able to exert an influence on the political life of the continent out of all proportion to their size.

They are dependent to a large extent for supplies, equipment and training on foreign help—most of it from the capitalist world. In 1964, there were 3,000 French and 600 British military experts in Africa; 1,500 Africans were sent to France for military training, and 700 to Britain. Some fourteen African states have agreements with Israel for the training of armies and for the supply of arms. Recently, the Federal Republic of Germany has concluded agreements for the provision of experts and other forms of military "aid" with seven African states in the major strategic areas of Africa. Meantime, the U.S.A., as its business interests develop in Africa, is stepping up its military and intelligence network, thereby exerting heavy pressures in the political sphere.

As long as African states continue to be dependent in any degree for training, and for arms and supplies on capitalist sources, the African Revolution is in jeopardy. It is not without significance that there have been no coups in countries where expatriate officers still exist in the armed forces. Although relatively small in numbers they are able to prevent any change in the status quo by virtue of the fact that they represent the military strength of the foreign power on whom the indigenous government depends for its security.

8

COUPS D'ETAT

Coups d'état are forms of struggle, the objective being the seizure of political power. Though carried out by a special organ of the state apparatus seemingly isolated from society, they reflect class interests and are part of the class struggle and the struggle between capitalism and socialist revolution. They do not change the nature or the content of the struggle; they only change its form. The politico-economic and social situation is in essence unchanged, since revolutionary needs remain unsatisfied. Reactionary coups actually accelerate the impetus towards socialist revolution, because objective conditions which generate revolution continue and gain momentum.

Reactionary, pro-imperialist coups signify that imperialism and its internal allies, being unable to thwart the advance of the masses and to defeat the socialist revolution by traditional methods, have resorted to the use of arms. They reveal the desperation and weakness of the reactionary forces, not their strength. They are the last ditch stand by indigenous exploiting classes and neocolonialists to preserve the bourgeois reactionary status quo.

All manner of reasons have been given by bourgeois observers to explain the causes of the succession of coups which have taken place in Africa in recent years. In some cases, coups have been attributed to tribalism and regionalism. Others are said to have occurred because of the disgust of elements among the armed forces and police with the ineptitude and corruption of politicians and the "economic chaos" they have caused. Not one of these explanations accords with the true facts. Those who put forward these and similar explanations, have made a superficial and distorted analysis of the actual situation. They are seemingly blind to the class struggle and the part played by bourgeois class interests and neocolonialist pressures. Even more important, they practically ignore the repressive nature of the coup and the virtually total non-participation of the vast majority of the population. Yet once the coup has taken place, the masses are always said to have welcomed it with "great enthusiasm". Carefully arranged "demonstrations" take place which are said to be positive proof that the coup-makers represent the will of the population as a whole. At the same time, the reactionary cliques who have seized power, and who represent only narrow bourgeois class interests, proceed to set up so-called "revolutionary" or "liberation" councils. By the use of such terms the people are expected to believe that the new regime is liberating them and fulfilling their revolutionary aspirations.

In the case of revolutionary nationalist coups, those who seize power assert that they do so in order to banish foreign politico-economic dominance. In this, they may be said to be acting in the interests of the people as a whole. But the revolution is not socialist. It springs from—and represents action by—the nationalist bourgeoisie. The position of workers and peasants after revolutionary nationalist coups is scarcely affected. They continue to be exploited and oppressed, this time by the indigenous bourgeoisie with foreign business interests more concealed than ever behind a façade of nationalisation policies.

At present, there is in Africa an intensification of struggles and conflicts between imperialism and its class allies on the one hand, and the vast mass of the African peoples on the other. Imperialist aggression has expressed itself not only in coups d'état, but in the assassination of revolutionary leaders, and the setting up of new intelligence organisations. In addition, there has been an intensification of already-existing western capitalist intelligence networks which work in close co-operation with neocolonialist governments to block socialist advance. Most prominent and active in Africa are those of the

U.S.A., Britain, West Germany, France, Israel, Portugal, Rhodesia and South Africa.

Most of these intelligence organisations work in close collaboration with one another in spheres where their vital interests are concerned. And in many cases they are behind coups d'état. This can be seen by the fact that coups d'état do not occur in regimes where army, police and intelligence networks are administered by European officers of the ex-colonial power. These ex-colonial bureaucrats see to it that coups d'état do not take place because they know that the neocolonialist puppet government is in fact the instrument of the neocolonialist power whose interests they are there to serve and guard.

Further, there has been a stepping up of military and politico-economic co-ordination between the members of the White Triangle in Africa—Portugal, Rhodesia and South Africa. On the other hand, recent years have shown a tremendous upsurge in African socialist revolutionary activity. This is evident in the growing resistance of workers and peasants to reactionary regimes, and in the mounting guerilla movements all over the African continent.

Within six years, between January 1963 and December 1969, twenty-five coups d'état have taken place in Africa:

Date	Place
13th January 1963	Togo
12th–15th August 1963	Congo, Brazzaville
19th–28th October	Dahomey
18th February 1964	Gabon
1st January 1965	Central African Republic
4th January 1965	Upper Volta
18th June 1965	Algeria
25th November 1965	Congo, Kinshasa

Time	Place
22nd December 1965	Dahomey
15th January 1966	Nigeria
24th February 1966	Ghana
29th July 1966	Nigeria
29th November 1966	Burundi
13th January 1967	Togo
24th March 1967	Sierra Leone
17th December 1967	Dahomey
18th April 1968	Sierra Leone
3rd August 1968	Congo, Brazzaville
4th September 1968	Congo, Brazzaville
19th November 1968	Mali
25th May 1969	Sudan
1st September 1969	Libya
15th–19th October 1969	Somalia
10th December 1969	Dahomey
30th January 1970	Lesotho

Apart from these, there have been innumerable attempted coups and assassinations. In January 1964, mutinies occurred among the armies of Tanzania, Uganda and Kenya. These were suppressed with the aid of British troops. In other independent states, plots and attempted coups have been exposed and foiled.

The very nature of the politico-economic relationship between neocolonialism and puppet regimes in a Balkanised Africa means that coups d'état will continue to take place in

Africa until the political unification of the African continent has been achieved.

Underlying every coup or attempted coup there is a similar basic situation. On the one hand, there are the neocolonialist powers teleguiding and supporting the neocolonialist state and power struggles within the reactionary bourgeois power elites; and on the other hand, there are the awakening African masses revealing the growing strength of the African socialist revolution. The African masses, when political independence was achieved, did not for a time discern the hidden hand of neocolonialism cleverly concealed behind the newly-independent government. But their awareness is growing, and is seen as a threat to the entrenched position of the indigenous bourgeoisie and their neocolonial masters. These have become alarmed by the increasing momentum of guerilla activity. Guerilla bases exist throughout Africa.

There is not one country in Africa today where the political consciousness of the worker-peasant class has resulted in the establishment of a socialist state. In each of the independent states are to be found the government and its ruling party; the bourgeois nationalist class; and the worker-peasant class. In many cases, the bourgeois nationalist class is involved perceptibly or imperceptibly with the ruling party and therefore the government. Where the bourgeois nationalist party does not form part of the government and the party, it plans subversion and organises coups.

The worker-peasant class even though it has assisted in the winning of independence, has not yet assumed leadership in Africa as a conscious class. In almost every African state, nonindependent and independent, guerilla struggle is being prepared or has been established as the only means to overthrow colonialist, neocolonialist, or settler regimes. Some of the guerilla liberation struggles are led by genuine socialist revolutionaries. Others are under the direction of members of the national bourgeoisie, who aim to free their territories from the foreigner, but who do not seek to establish a socialist state. They constitute a potential threat to the African Revolution, since the total liberation and the political unification of Africa can only be finally accomplished through the adoption of scientific socialism.

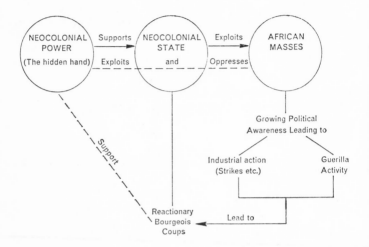

The following liberation movements are the most notable at present engaged in guerilla operations:

South Africa:

PAC: Pan Africanist Congress.
ANC: African National Congress.
APDUSA: African People's Democratic Union of Southern Africa.

Zimbabwe (*Rhodesia*).

ZANU: Zimbabwe African National Union.
ZAPU: Zimbabwe African People's Union.

South West Africa:

SWAPO: South West African People's Organisation.
SWANU: South West African National Union.

Angola:

MPLA: Popular Movement for the Liberation of Angola.
GRAE: Revolutionary Government of Angola in Exile.
UNITA: National Union for the Total Independence of Angola.

Mozambique:

FRELIMO: Front for the Liberation of Mozambique.
COREMO: Revolutionary Committee of Mozambique.

Portuguese Guinea:

PAIGC: African Party for the Independence of Guinea and Cape Verde Islands.

CHAD:

FROLINA: Front for National Liberation

CONGO, KINSHASA:

CNL: Congolese National Liberation Movement

ERITREA:

ELF: Eritrean Liberation Front

Guerilla activities will also continue in many of the independent African states, so long as there is no attempt being made to have the means of production owned by the masses of the African people. Unless the leaders of the independent African states stop paying lip service to socialism and go all out for scientific socialism they are only deferring the guerilla onset. At present guerilla activities are proceeding in Gabon, Ethiopia, Malawi, Sudan, Eritrea, Kenya, Cameroun, Niger, Ivory Coast, etc. The wind of guerilla struggle is blowing all over Africa and will not stop until Africa is united under socialism.

In the face of the growing political awareness of the masses, reactionary governments either attempt to contain it by introducing bogus socialist policies, to suppress it by force, or to carry out a military coup. Whichever method is adopted, they proclaim that they are serving the interests of the people by getting rid of corrupt and inefficient politicians, and that they are putting the economy in order. They are, in fact, safeguarding capitalism and protecting their own bourgeois interests and the interests of foreign monopoly finance capital.

The rash of military coups in Africa reveals the lack of socialist revolutionary organisation, the need for the founding of an all-African vanguard working-class party, and for the creation of an all-African peoples' army and militia. Socialist revolutionary struggle, whether in the form of political, economic or military action, can only be ultimately effective if it is organised, and if it has its roots in the class struggle of workers and peasants.

9

BOURGEOISIE

Colonialism, imperialism and neocolonialism are expressions of capitalism and of bourgeois economic and political aspirations. In Africa, under colonialism, capitalist development led to the decline of feudalism and to the emergence of new class structures.

Before the colonial period, the power of the chiefs—which was generally not based on land ownership—was strictly limited and controlled. The "stool" and not the chief was sacred. Control was exercised by a council of elders. Colonialism reinforced the power of chiefs through the system of "Indirect Rule". They were given new powers, were sometimes paid, and became for the most part the local agents of colonialism. In some colonised areas new chiefs were appointed by the colonial power. These became known as "warrant chiefs".

Imperialists utilised the feudal and tribal nobility to support their exploitation; and this resulted in a blunting of social contradictions, since the feudal and semi-feudal strata maintained a strong hold over the peasant masses and inhibited the growth of revolutionary organisations.

Relics of feudalism still exist in many parts of Africa. For example, in Northern Nigeria and in North and West Cameroun, tribal chiefs live on the exploitation of peasants who not only have to pay them tributes and taxes, but who often have to do forced labour.

But although feudal relics remain, the colonial period ushered in capitalist social structures. The period was characterised by the rise of the petty bourgeoisie, and of a small but influential national bourgeoisie consisting in the main of intellectuals, civil servants, members of the professions, and of officers in the armed forces and police. There was a marked absence of capitalists among the bourgeoisie, since local business enterprise was on the whole discouraged by the colonial power. Anyone wishing to achieve wealth and status under colonialism was therefore likely to choose a career in the professions, the civil service or the armed forces, because there were so few business opportunities. Foreigners controlled mining, industrial enterprises, banks, wholesale trade and large-scale farming. In most of Africa, the bourgeoisie was, in fact, for the most part petty bourgeoisie.

It was partly the restrictions placed on the business outlets of the African bourgeoisie which led it to oppose imperialist rule. After the end of the Second World War, when the pressure for national liberation was increased, imperialists were compelled to admit part of the African bourgeoisie to spheres from which it had previously been excluded. More Africans were allowed into the state machinery and into foreign companies. Thus, a new African elite, closely linked with foreign capital, was created. At the same time, repressive measures were taken against progressive parties and trade unions. Several colonialist wars were fought, as for example, the wars against the peoples of Madagascar, Cameroun and Algeria. It was during this period that the foundations of neocolonialism were laid.

During the national liberation struggle, the petty bourgeoisie tends to divide into three main categories. Firstly, there are those who are heavily committed to colonialism and to capitalist economic and social development. These are in the main the "officials" and professional men, and agents of foreign firms and companies. Secondly, there are the "revolutionary" petty bourgeoisie—the nationalists—who want to end colonial rule but who do not wish to see a transformation of society. They form part of the national bourgeoisie. Thirdly, there are those who "sit on the fence", and are prepared to be passive onlookers.

In general, few members of the African bourgeoisie amassed sufficient capital to become significant in the business sector. The African bourgeoisie remains therefore largely a comprador class, sharing in some of the profits which imperialism drains from Africa. Under conditions of colonialism and neo-colonialism, it will never be encouraged sufficiently to become strong in the economic sphere since this would mean creating business competitors. The local bourgeoisie must always be subordinate partners to foreign capitalism. For this reason, it cannot achieve power as a class or govern without the close support of reactionary feudal elements within the country, or without the political, economic and military support of international capitalism.

Imperialism may foster liberation movements in colonial areas when capitalist exploitation has reached the stage of giving rise to a labour movement which seriously threatens the interests of international capitalism. By the granting of political independence to bourgeois Parties, reactionary indigenous forces can thereby be put into positions of power which enable them to cement their alliance with the international bourgeoisie. In practically every national liberation struggle, there emerge two liberation Parties. One of them is the genuine peoples' Party, committed not only to national liberation but to socialism. The other aims at political independence, but intends to preserve capitalist structures, and is supported by imperialism.

In the majority of the independent African states there exist embryonic elements of a rural bourgeoisie. In Ghana, large farmers and cocoa brokers come into this category. According to the 1960 census, the rural bourgeoisie number 1.4 million, while the urban middle class was estimated at 300,000. This was in a population 24 per cent of which was defined as urban. In most cases, both urban and rural bourgeoisie are not conscious of themselves as a class, though they are very much aware of their strength and importance, and conscious of the threat to their privileged positions in society by the increasing pressure of worker-peasant resistance.

In the struggle for political independence, urban workers, peasants and the national bourgeoisie, ally together to eject the colonial power. Class cleavages are temporarily blurred. But once independence is achieved, class conflicts come to the fore over the social and economic policies of the new government.

It is possible for classes to combine in the post-colonial situation, and the nature of the government is assessed by which particular class interests are dominant. Theorists arguing that proletariat and petty bourgeoisie should join together to win the peasantry, in order to attack the bourgeoisie, ignore the fact that the petty bourgeoisie will always, when it comes to the pinch, side with the bourgeoisie to preserve capitalism. It is only peasantry and proletariat working together who are wholly able to subscribe to policies of all-out socialism. Where conflict involves both political and economic interests, the economic always prevails.

The African bourgeoisie, in common with their counterpart in other parts of the world, hold the view that governments exist to protect private property, and that success is measured by wealth, the acquisition of property and social status. They set up bourgeois organisations such as clubs and professional associations on the model of those existing in the bourgeois societies of Europe and the Americas. They want politics to be confined to the struggles between various propertied groups. It is common in Africa, and in other coup areas of the world—notably Asia and Latin America—for there to be a succession of bourgeois coups d'état in a single state. The propertied fight the propertied for political supremacy. For the independent states of Africa, Asia and Latin America have a similar historical past in that they have suffered from imperialism and colonialism; and after political independence have in almost every case, been swept into the orbit of neo-colonialism. In this situation, the majority are governed by bourgeois elements who compete among themselves for political domination. For whichever group succeeds in dominating the political scene is in a position to enhance its property and status. Other factors such as regionalism and tribalism obviously enter into the struggle for power among the indigenous bourgeoisie, but the essential point remains, that these struggles take place among the propertied class, and are not struggles between classes.

The tribal formula is frequently used to obscure the class forces created in African society by colonialism. In many areas, uneven economic development under colonial rule led to a differentiation of economic functions along ethnic lines. This tendency is exploited in the interests of international capitalism.

A distinction must be made between tribes and tribalism. The clan is the extended family, and the tribe is the extended clan with the same ethnic language within a territory. There were tribes in Africa before imperialist penetration, but no "tribalism" in the modern sense. Tribalism arose from colonialsim, which exploited feudal and tribal survivals to combat the growth of national liberation movements.

The formation of nationalities was retarded as a result of colonial conquest, when the imperialists carved up Africa among themselves, disregarding geographical, linguistic and ethnic realities. The normal growth of the economy and of the class structure of African society was hindered and distorted. Patriarchal and feudal structures were artificially preserved, and all possible obstacles erected to prevent the emergence of a class-conscious proletariat.

Capitalist methods of exploitation inevitably gave birth to a proletariat, particularly in areas where mines and plantations were highly developed, as in South and East Africa, and in Congo Kinshasa. Here, workers were kept in tribal or traditional structures, and in reservations, in an attempt to prevent the growth of class consciousness.

At Independence, the colonial powers again fostered separatism and tribal differences through the encouragement of federal constitutions. Genuine independence was prevented through the operation of diverse forms of neocolonialism.

In the era of neocolonialism, tribalism is exploited by the bourgeois ruling classes as an instrument of power politics, and as a useful outlet for the discontent of the masses. Many of the so-called tribal conflicts in modern Africa are in reality class forces brought into conflict by the transition from colonialism to neocolonialism. Tribalism is the result, not the cause, of underdevelopment. In the majority of "tribal" conflicts, the source is the exploiting bourgeois or feudal minority in co-operation with imperialists and neocolonialists seeking to promote their joint class interests. Support has tended to be withdrawn from traditional rulers and transferred to the rising urban bourgeoisie who are, under neocolonialism, in a better position to maintain and promote the interests of international capitalism. The process assumes the appearance of a tribal confrontation, but in reality is part of the class struggle.

The emergence of tribes in any country is natural, or due to historical development. Tribes, like nationalities may always remain in a country, but it is tribalism—tribal politics—that should be fought and destroyed. Under a socialist Union Government of Africa, tribalism, not tribes, will disappear.

Certain elements among the African bourgeoisie and traditional rulers—for example, revolutionary intellectuals—may dissociate themselves from their class origin and the ideology connected with it. These are "revolutionary outsiders", who can be absorbed into the ranks of the socialist revolution.

For the most part, however, in areas of the world where capitalist development is in its infancy, the bourgeoisie—heavily outnumbered by peasantry and proletariat—feel threatened by the rising tide of socialism. As a result, there is a close drawing together of bourgeois elite groupings, and special reliance is placed on the military. Neocolonialist, bourgeois military coups take place to forestall or to destroy the power of workers and peasants, and of socialist-oriented governments.

Such coups are strongly supported by the machinery of neocolonialism. For imperialists and neocolonialists seek, in their own interests, to support the privileged class which emerged under colonialism. Both indigenous bourgeoisie and neocolonialists have common interests in prolonging their dominance by preserving the fundamental features of the colonial state apparatus. The bureaucratic bourgeoisie, in particular, is the spoilt child of neocolonialist governments. Many African states spend ridiculously large sums of money on their bureaucrats. For example, Gabon, with a population of less than half a million has a Parliament of 65 members, each earning

165,000 francs a year. Yet the average worker in Gabon earns only 700 francs annually. In Dahomey, 60 per cent of the national income is spent on paying the salaries of government officials.

The bureaucratic bourgeoisie, the inheritors of the functions of earlier ruling classes, are closely connected with foreign firms, with the diplomats of imperialist countries, and with the African exploiting classes. Although not a cohesive elite, they

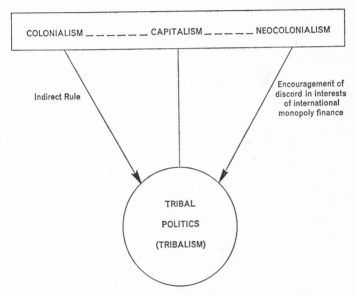

are in general dedicated to the capitalist path of development, and are among the most devoted of indigenous agents of neo-colonialism. Their education and class position largely isolate them from the masses.

At Independence, their position is strengthened immeasur-ably by the Africanisation policies of the newly-independent government, and by the tremendous increase of work entailed in the large scale economic and social planning undertaken by the new government. They provide the administrative and

61

technical expertise required. Further, they are able to select and organise the information to be laid before ministers responsible for the formulation of policy. In this way, they play a considerable part in actual decision-making. Many top bureaucrats assume responsibilities and powers for which they are not equipped. They tend to become arrogant and isolated from the lower strata of civil servants and clerks, and submissive to foreign, neocolonialist bureaucrats. When they exert influence on policy it is likely to be along class lines. Their education and class position make them separate from the masses, and they become the willing accomplices of local capitalists, dishonest intellectuals, ambitious army and police officers, and of neocolonialists. Although subject always to the control of a political and military authority, they occupy an extremely strong position in the neocolonialist state apparatus, and exert their influence in support of the ruling classes. They become in some cases, particularly under military-police dictatorships, the de facto policy makers, without being answerable to the public. This becomes particularly apparent when they act in league with foreign bureaucrats.

When reactionary military coups take place, whether or not they have been involved in planning them, they readily support the bourgeois coup-makers by carrying on the day to day work of administration, and by assisting in the drawing up and carrying out of decrees and regulations. Top bureaucrats sit on the innumerable councils, commissions of inquiry and so on which proliferate after a coup. In effect, the establishment of arbitrary military-police rule enhances their position since the reactionary new rulers are utterly dependent on them. Unlike "civilian governments", military regimes are in a position to impose policies without having to obtain the consent of the peoples' representatives. They can, therefore, allow bureaucrats much greater freedom of action.

Top civil servants assist in policy making in most countries. In the U.S.A., they change with a change of government and are very much a part of the decision-making power elite. In Britain, they are supposed to be apolitical and to serve whichever government is in power.

But in Africa, the bourgeoisie as a whole cannot be seen in isolation from imperialism, colonialism and neocolonialism. While representing only a very small fraction of the population it is nevertheless a great danger to the African masses because of the strength it derives from its dependence on foreign bourgeois capitalism which seeks to keep the peasants and workers of Africa in a condition of perpetual subjection.

It is, in fact, impossible to separate the interests of the African bourgeoisie and those of international monopoly finance capital. The weakening of either one of them inevitably results in the weakening of the other.

The alliance between the indigenous bourgeoisie and international monopoly finance capital is being further cemented by the growing trend towards partnership between individual African governments, or regional economic organisations, and giant, imperialist, multi-national corporations. African governments, some of which claim to be pursuing a socialist path of development and "nationalising" key industries, are in fact merely "participating" in them. They are combining with collective imperialism in the continuing exploitation of African workers and rural proletariat. The African government shields the corporations from the resistance of the working class, and bans strikes or becomes the strike-breaker; while the corporations strengthen their stranglehold of the African economy, secure in the knowledge that they have government protection. In fact, the African governments become the policemen of imperialist, multi-national corporations. There thus develops a common front to halt socialist advance.

It is the indigenous bourgeoise who provide the main means by which international monopoly finance continues to plunder Africa and to frustrate the purposes of the African Revolution. The exposure and the defeat of the African bourgeoisie, therefore, provides the key to the successful accomplishment of the worker-peasant struggle to achieve total liberation and socialism, and to advance the cause of the entire world socialist revolution.

10

PROLETARIAT

A modern proletariat already exists in Africa, though it is relatively small in size. This is the class base for the building of socialism, and must be seen in the context of the international working-class movement from which it derives much of its strength.

The emergence of the working class in Africa is associated with colonialism and with foreign capital. In most areas, the size of the proletariat remained small because of the lack of large scale industrialisation. However, in countries with most developed economies, such as Egypt and South Africa, a strong working class emerged. It was in these countries, in the 1920s, where Africa's first communist parties, consisting of workers, peasants and intellectuals were formed. At about the same time, communist parties linked with the French Communist Party, were founded in Algeria, Morocco and Tunisia.

By the mid-1950s, Africa had more than ten million wage workers. Some 50 per cent of all persons in paid employment were engaged in agriculture; 40 per cent in industry and transport; and 10 per cent in civil service and in trading establishments. By 1962, it is estimated that there were 15 million workers in Africa, representing about 6 to 7 per cent of the whole population. While this percentage may appear very small, for example compared with Asia where workers are said to number approximately 100 million, it must be assessed by its performance and its potential, and in solidarity with world proletarian movements.

African workers played an important role in national liberation struggles. By strike action they succeeded in disrupting economic life and caused great embarrassment to the colonial administration. There were general strikes in Kenya, Nigeria, Ghana and Guinea in the years leading up to independence. In addition, there were throughout colonial Africa innumerable strikes which affected particular sectors of the economy. The Rand miners' strike of 1946, and the strikes in the Tanganyika sisal industry between 1957–9 are typical examples. During these strikes, and others equally effective but far too numerous to list, mass feeling was awakened, and workers became to some extent conscious of themselves as a class.

South Africa is probably the most urbanised part of Africa. In 1966 it is estimated that there were about seven million African workers living in the towns. It is because of this that some theorists argue it is possible to by-pass the stage of bourgeois democracy in South Africa and to proceed straight to socialism. An interesting consideration in this respect, is the fact that in China, the industrial working class was only one per cent of the population before the Communist Revolution. Liberation armies were based largely on the peasantry. At present, the industrial working class of China is only about 3 per cent of the total population.

It is the task of the African urban proletariat to win the peasantry to revolution by taking the revolution to the countryside. For the most part, the peasantry are as yet unorganised, and unrevolutionary. Large numbers are illiterate. But once both urban proletariat and peasants join forces in the struggle to achieve socialism, the African Revolution has in effect been won. For the African bourgeoisie and their imperialist and neocolonialist masters cannot successfully resist their overwhelming combined strength.

In many of the African independent states, the absence of large-scale industry, and the relatively low skill and educational standards of the workers retards class consciousness. They are often non-revolutionary, and have a petty bourgeois mentality. Yet in Senegal, for example, where the working class is larger than in many other African states, and where there is 95 per cent illiteracy among male workers, and 99 per cent among women, there is a vigorous working class movement.

65

Under colonialism, the workers' struggle was largely directed against the foreign exploiter. It was in this sense more an anti-colonial, than a class struggle. It has, furthermore, strong racial undertones. This class-race aspect of the African workers' struggle remains under conditions of neocolonialism, and tends to blunt the awareness of the workers to the existence of indigenous bourgeois exploitation. The workers' attack is directed against Europeans, Lebanese, Indians and others, while the indigenous reactionary exploiter is overlooked.

In neocolonialist states where there are immigrant workers, and where unemployment is rife, a similar situation develops. The anger of workers is surreptitiously fomented and directed by the neocolonialist puppet regime not so much against its own reactionary policies as against the "alien" workers. It is they who are blamed for the scarcity of jobs, the shortage of houses, rising prices and so on. The result is that the African immigrant worker is victimised both by the government and by his own fellow workers. The government brings in measures to restrict immigration, to limit the opportunities of existing immigrants, and to expel certain categories. The indigenous workers, for their part, are led to believe by the government's action, that the cause of unemployment and bad living conditions is attributable in large measure to the presence of immigrant workers. Mass feeling against them is aroused, and helps to increase any already existing national and ethnic animosities. Instead of joining with immigrant workers to bring pressure on the government, many of them strongly support measures taken against them. In this they show lack of awareness of the class nature of the struggle; and the bourgeoisie benefit from the split among the ranks of the working class.

Workers are workers, and nationality, race, tribe and religion are irrelevancies in the struggle to achieve socialism.

In the context of the African socialist revolution there is no justification for regarding non-African workers as a hindrance to economic progress, and there is similarly no justification for the victimisation and the expulsion of migrant African labour from one territory to another. In Africa there should be no African "alien". All are Africans. The enemy-wall to be brought down and crushed is not the African "alien" worker but Balkanisation and the artificial territorial boundaries created by imperialism.

The migrant urban population can be a very powerful force for the spread of revolutionary socialism. The many workers who go to the cities and to other African countries to work for a period of time and then return to their homes, link the revolutionary movements of the proletariat with the countryside and with the labour movements of other states. They are an indispensable part of the revolutionary process, and the permanent mobility of the African labour force must be encouraged and organised.

Large scale migrations of people is a feature of Africa. There is on the one hand, the migration of country folk to the towns, and on the other hand, the migration of labour from one country to another. Towns are largely the product of external forces. They developed, in the main, as a result of the market economy introduced by European colonialism. Among the reasons for the migration from the countryside to the towns, are the search for employment; the desire for cash to buy manufactured goods, and to pay for the education of children; and the wish to enjoy the many amenities of town life.

There has in recent years been a great increase in the urban population of Africa. For example, the figures below show the rate of growth in three of Ghana's main cities:

	Year	Population (figures are approximate)
Accra	1936	38,000
	1960	338,000
Kumasi	1921	24,000
	1966	190,000
Tamale	1921	4,000
	1960	40,000

Broadly, the class structure of African towns may be said to include, the bourgeois class of professional, intellectual, bureaucratic, military, business, political and managerial elites; the schoolteachers, clergy, small business men, executives in government departments, shopkeepers; and the lower middle class strata of junior clerks, artisans, tradesmen and semi-skilled workers. Secondly, there is the working class, comprising the broad mass of petty traders, manual workers, market women, and migrant labourers. Finally, there are what may be described as the "déclassés". These are the beggars, prostitutes and general layabouts who form the lumpen-proletariat; and those—mostly young people—connected with petty bourgeois or workers' families, who go to the towns from the rural areas, and who usually do no work but live at the expense of their families. These young people may play an important part in the liberation struggle. They are in touch with both town and countryside, and may become effective revolutionary cadres.

Members of the bourgeois elites mix freely in clubs and societies, which cut across race and emphasise social class. The existence of class feeling is shown in the desire of many to join associations which will enhance status. The higher the educational qualification, the higher the status and opportunities for top level employment, an overseas education being rated the highest qualification of all.

The migrant labourers bring with them their own social strata, ideologies, religions and customs. Some of them become completely submerged and absorbed within the local population. But relatively few settle permanently. The vast majority work for a few years and then return to their native home. According to the 1960 census in Ghana, only 25 per cent of the population of Takoradi were of local origin. In Kumasi the figure was 37 per cent. In Sekondi, 40 per cent only were of local origin. In 1948, over half the population of Takoradi, and 36 per cent in the case of Accra, had lived in those towns for less than five years. It is estimated that some 40 per cent of wage earners in Ghana are migrants.

Though the percentage of migrant labour among urban population elsewhere in Africa may differ substantially, wherever immigrant labourers exist they represent a vast mobile force which can become a vital factor in the African socialist revolution. They can assist the integration of workers in the revolutionary struggle and infiltrate every sector of the neo-colonialist and bourgeois economy.

Under conditions of neocolonialism, migrant labour tends to retard the development of class consciousness and to hinder the growth of workers' organisations. Migrant labourers form their own tribal associations, which are mainly benefit societies.

Yet there was a big expansion of trade unionism in Africa after the Second World War. In many countries, trade unions participated actively in the liberation struggle, organising strikes, boycotts and other industrial action. The development of trade union militancy was vigorously opposed by the colonial powers who tried, and sometimes succeeded in eroding the leadership by reformism, and the infiltration of Right-wing socialist ideas.

In May 1961, on the initiative of trade unions in Ghana, Guinea and Mali, the All-African Trade Union Congress was held in Casablanca, at which 45 trade union organisations and 38 countries were represented. The All-African Trade Union Federation (A.A.T.U.F.) was set up, founded on the principles of proletariat solidarity and internationalism. A rival trade union organisation, the African Trade Union Congress (A.T.U.C.), was founded in January 1962, as the result of a conference held in Dakar attended by delegates from African organisations affiliated with the International Confederation of Free Trade Unions, and eight independent trade union organisations. No mention was made in the Charter of the Confederation of African Trade Unions of either foreign monopolies or proletariat internationalism.

The African trade union movement must be organised on a pan-African scale, be genuinely socialist oriented, and developed as an integral part of the African workers' class struggle. For this purpose, an All-African Trade Union Congress must be established to co-ordinate and direct trade union activity throughout the entire African continent. It must be quite separate from the trade union organisations of other countries, though work at the international level in close association with them.

Urbanisation is at the core of social change. Therefore, industrialisation, which is the main cause of urban growth, determines the social pattern. With growing industrialisation, the African proletariat will increase in numbers and become more class conscious.

At present, Africa is industrially one of the least developed continents in the world. It produces one-seventh of the world's raw materials, but only one-fiftieth of the world's manufactures. The share of industry in Africa's total income is less than 14 per cent. This situation is a legacy of imperialism and colonialism, and the exploitation of Africa to serve the interests of international monopoly finance capital. But it is also a result of the continuing imperialist and capitalist exploitation of Africa through neocolonialism.

Western monopolies still dominate about 80 per cent of the volume of African trade. A significant factor in recent times has been the rapid development of U.S. penetration:

	1950	*1960*	*1964*
Investments:	$287 million	$925 million	$1,700 million
Exports from *U.S.A. to Africa:*	$494 million		$916 million
Imports from *Africa:*	$362 million		$1,211 million

Between 1951–1955, direct U.S. investments in Africa increased more than 2·5 times—from $313 million to $793 million. Particularly deep penetration was made into South Africa, Rhodesia and Congo Kinshasa.

The methods of neocolonialism are economic control, in the form of "aid", "loans", trade and banking; the stranglehold of indigenous economies through vast international interlocking corporations; political direction through puppet governments; social penetration through the cultivation of an indigenous bourgeoisie, the imposition of "defence" agreements, and the setting up of military and air bases; ideological expansion through the mass communications media of press, radio and television—the emphasis being on anti-Communism; the fomenting of discord between countries and tribes; and through collective imperialism—notably the politico-economic and military co-operation of Rhodesia, South Africa and Portugal.

Neocolonialism, by its very nature, cannot overcome its own problems and contradictions. Imperialism is moribund capitalism; neocolonialism is moribund colonialism. Both sharpen the contradictions in their nature, which eventually lead to their destruction. Neocolonialism cannot prop up the governments of the "new bourgeoisie", and promote stable economic development when the objective is profit for the foreign investor. Therefore, the indigenous bourgeoisie can never become a really safe governing class, and the need arises for more and more forceful intervention from external interests, and repression from within. This state of affairs accelerates the emergence of a really revolutionary class struggle.

The granting of economic "aid" from capitalist countries is one of the most insidious ways in which neocolonialism hinders economic progress in the developing world, retarding industrialisation and delaying the development of a large proletariat. Only 10 per cent of U.S. "aid" to Africa is spent on industrialisation, and most of this is in those areas regarded as "safe" for capitalism. In contrast, 70 per cent of aid from socialist countries is spent on industrialisation and the organisation of profitable production. Interest rates on loans from capitalist countries vary from between $6\frac{1}{2}$ to 8 per cent, whereas socialist creditors charge only $2\frac{1}{2}$ per cent. Aid from socialist countries is used mainly for state projects. This again is in striking contrast to "aid" from the West, which is almost entirely in the private sector.

France spends something like two thousand million francs on "aid" to the francophone countries in Africa. These two thousand million are the means by which France maintains very close cultural, political and economic ties with them, for they are large markets for French exports. In fact, the "aid" is considered by French governments to be "good investment".

A considerable proportion of money disbursed as bilateral "aid" from the West either does not leave the donor country at all, the "aid" being provided in the form of goods, or returns in a relatively short period as payment for additional exports, or in other ways. Of every £100 of bilateral "aid" disbursed by the U.K. in the period 1964–66, £72·5 was "aid" tied to the supply of British goods, or resulted in direct spending on British goods and services.

Multilateral "aid" similarly serves mainly to improve the economic position of the donor countries. It has been estimated that the U.K. has secured export orders of over £116 for every £100 of its multilateral "aid", due largely to the operations of the International Development Agency (I.D.A.). For example, a recent Whitehall study on the subject has calculated that for every £100 contributed to I.D.A. by the U.K. in 1964–66, I.D.A. spent about £150 on U.K. goods. Indeed, many projects accomplished through foreign "aid" are designed to help the donor's balance of payments rather than the recipient's economic development. The recipient is burdened not only with a costly loan to repay, but also sometimes with uneconomic projects, and with political and economic strings which hamper independent development, and positively retard economic growth.

Credits are granted by capitalist states to countries of Africa, Asia and Latin America, so that they can be equipped with the infra-structure necessary for their further exploitation by private monopolists. The aim is political as well as economic. It seeks to block socialist advance by winning over the indigenous bourgeoisie, by giving them an interest in the business; and at the same time to extend the stranglehold of international monopoly finance on the economies of the developing world.

The rural proletariat—small farmers and plantation workers producing cotton, sisal, cocoa, coffee, rubber, citrus fruits and other crops, which bring them within the orbit of international trade and industry, are strategic links in the chain of African proletariat struggle. Imperialism in its neocolonialist phase, however, draws the bulk of its profits from its grip over the advanced sectors of production such as mining, manufacturing, commerce, retail trade, fisheries, and transport. About 90 per cent of all western capital invested in Africa is sunk into enterprises connected with these sectors, and it is in these key sectors where the industrial proletariat—the indispensable labour force for the continued existence of neocolonialism—is in a position to spearhead the socialist revolution.

Attempts have been made to deny the existence of a working class in Africa. In areas where it has been impossible to ignore its existence—such as the mining areas of South Africa, Congo Kinshasa and Zambia—strenuous efforts have been made to integrate it within the neocolonialist, capitalist system of exploitation. This is done by fostering the growth of trade unions under reformist leadership, and by granting a certain measure of "welfare" benefits. In some parts of Africa, specially in the highly developed mining areas, Africanisation policies are pursued to placate workers, and wages and salaries of Africans are brought closer to expatriate levels. This has had the effect in some cases of making the workers less likely to indulge in revolutionary activities.

The tendency in the transitional period between capitalism and socialism is embourgeoisement. The working class vision of socialism during this period may be blurred by the corruption of the "welfare state". In these conditions, the worker becomes a well fed Philistine and turns towards reaction and conservatism. Socialist revolution then becomes a minor issue.

Economically and industrially, Europe and the U.S.A. are ready and poised for socialism. There are the necessary material ingredients which could make socialism possible overnight. In the U.S.A. when automation and cybernation aided by nuclear energy reach their highest form of development, the forces of production will have been developed to a point at which there could be the classless society which Marx predicted could come only under communism. But although the

U.S.A. is at present one of the most affluent and industrialised countries in the world, it is at the same time one of the most socially and politically backward.

A part of the working class of Europe and the U.S.A. had identified itself with capitalism. Strata of workers have become embourgeoised, and have thus weakened the working class forces for socialist revolution. In 1968, some ten million French workers went on strike and practically paralysed the government, and yet, they were unable to achieve revolutionary change.

Throughout the world, student protest has become an increasingly prominent feature of contemporary times. But students suffer a double alienation. They are alienated from the Establishment, and in many cases from their own families; but more important, they are alienated from the working class which should make use of their efforts in the revolutionary struggle.

In Britain, English manual workers who vote Conservative provide the Party with nearly half its electoral strength. Economic affluence, or status aspirations induce many members of the working class to claim middle class membership. In the so-called "welfare state", many working class live like the lower middle class. Economic satisfaction leads to middle class identification, which in its turn results in conservative voting.

In this situation, extension of voting rights to the mass of the population has not so much reduced the power of the ruling class, as caused the radicalism of the working class to decline. The tendency for some working class movements in capitalist societies to confine their activities only to trade unionism is a danger to socialist advance.

While conditions of embourgeoisement exist among the working class of capitalist countries an added responsibility rests on the exploited peoples of Africa, Asia and Latin America to promote the world's socialist revolution. In this process, the African proletariat has a vital and strategic part to play as the African Revolution gains momentum.

11

PEASANTRY

In Africa, the peasantry is by far the largest contingent of the working class, and potentially the main force for socialist revolution. But it is dispersed, unorganised, and for the most part unrevolutionary. It must be awakened and it must be led by its natural class allies—the proletariat and the revolutionary intelligentsia.

At the top of the class structure in rural areas are the traditional feudal landlords who live on the exploitation of the peasants; and the capitalist landlords—many of whom are absentee—who are dependent on the exploitation of wage labour. Among the latter—who form part of the rural bourgeoisie—are the clergy of various sects and religions who live on the feudal and capitalist exploitation of peasants. The rural bourgeoisie own relatively large farms. They own capital, exploit wage labour, and for the most part specialise in export or "cash" crops. The small farmers, who may be classed as petty rural bourgeoisie, possess little capital and cultivate land which they either own or rent. They employ members of their family or clan and/or wage labour. If the land is rented, the normal practice is for the petty farmer to retain about two-thirds of the proceeds of the farm for himself, and to pay one-third to the owner of the land. Below the petty rural bourgeoisie in the rural strata, are the peasants, those who cultivate negligible areas of land, and are often forced to sell their labour power to become seasonal workers. Finally, there are the agricultural labourers, the rural proletariat, who own nothing but their labour.

Thus the composition of the agrarian social strata consists of two major groups—the exploiting group and the exploited. These groups can each be sub-divided into smaller groups:

The *exploiting* classes consist of
(1) plantation owners
(2) "absentee" landlords
(3) farmers (comparatively large property owners)
(4) petty farmers.

The *exploited* classes are:
(1) peasants
(2) rural proletariat.

The plantation owners are for the most part aliens (e.g. U.A.C. in Nigeria, Cameroun and Congo Kinshasa and white minority settlers in South Africa and Rhodesia). These plantations are extensions of monopolies in Africa. The system of exploitation here conforms to the basic law of capitalism. The farm or plantation labourers are exploited. This exploitation of African workers is made possible by the low level of the standard of living of the workers which enables the monopolies to pay low nominal wages. But due to the ever rising prices of consumer goods, the real wages of these labourers are always declining. Hence the conflict between labour and capital is always grave. The foreign monopolies are alien absentee owners. But there also exist local absentee owners.

The local "absentee" landlords are mainly African land proprietors who live in the urban areas in luxury, while with the aid of capital, they control vast stretches of land in the rural areas. They live by exploiting the farm worker. The special peculiarity of exploitation applied here is that of payment in kind. Thus the farm labourer does not get guaranteed wages. He almost lives from hand to mouth. Hence the struggle between capital and labour here is as intense as that on the plantations. In many cases the absentee landlord also exploits the worker in the city through exorbitant house rents.

Another class in this sector of exploiters is the farmer. The farmer is normally an indigenous landowner, sometimes as large or larger than the "absentee" owner. Unlike the absentee owner he stays on the farm with his family. He is prosperous due to the fact that he owns fertile land, more farm implements and is therefore in a position to hire the labour of others. Farmers are always outstanding personalities in their respective areas, and usually have large families. Mostly, they are semi-feudal in methods of production, and sometimes also practise the system of payment in kind. They often owe allegiance to another big village chief or elder. The cultivation of export crops preoccupies them.

Just below the farmers in the rural social strata is the class of petty farmers. The petty farmer is a small property owner. He also owns a few implements and livestock. He is in the Marxist sense of revolutionary behaviour, unstable and vacillating. He mostly uses the labour of his family, and hires seasonal labour during times of tilling and harvest. He also aspires to become a prosperous farmer, to be able to maintain regular labourers and to own large property. Mostly he is preoccupied with the production of local products for home consumption.

The neighbour of the petty farmer is the peasant. The peasant is the smallest property owner. His life is governed by insecurity. He works a little land with or without livestock. He is largely dependent on natural forces; good weather brings him a favourable harvest; bad weather may ruin him and force him to become a paid agricultural labourer working on a large plantation or farm. Due to the ever rising cost of living, for example, soaring prices of manufactured goods, the difficulties of the peasant grow. He produces practically all he requires at home, and seldom requires exchange. The peasantry can be a revolutionary class if led by the urban and rural proletariat.

The rural proletariat are workers in the Marxist sense of the word. They are part of the working class and the most revolutionary of the African rural strata.

It is the revolutionary potential of the rural strata of peasants and agricultural labourers which must be developed for it is they who will provide the revolution with its main strength. It is the task of revolutionary cadres in the first place to awaken them to the realities of their economic potential, and to win them and the petty farmers over to socialist forms of organisation of agricultural production and distribution. This may be done through the development of various types of agricultural co-operatives, which are essential if the transition from private agriculture based on small-scale production to modern, mechanised, socialist agriculture is to be accomplished. Market co-operatives already operate in many African countries with great success; though credit co-operatives are less general, due to the shortage of funds. But by far the highest form of co-operation in agriculture is the production co-operative, which organises the administration and mechanism of agricultural production. This kind of co-operative is in its infancy, largely because of a lack of skilled personnel to operate it, and the scarcity of agricultural machinery. It can be abused if not supervised by a progressive government. Already, in neo-colonialist states, the co-operative movement largely serves the interests of the rural bourgeoisie and the monopoly capitalists. The neocolonialist elites exploit the relative isolation and cultural backwardness of the peasantry, and so induces it to accept their political dominance.

It is in the countryside where those feudal relics which still exist, are mainly to be found. In parts, the peasantry lives under conditions little different from pre-colonial and colonial periods. They bear heavy tax burdens, and in some areas are compelled to do forced labour. If they migrate to the towns they usually fall victim to colonial and neocolonial exploitation.

The African peasantry, like the peasantry of Asia and Latin America, has for a long time suffered from feudalism and from imperialist-capitalist exploitation. From Cairo to Cape Town and from the Cape Verde Islands to Kenya and Zanzibar the African peasant's situation and problems are practically the same. The peasantry must be liberated from semi-feudal and capitalist relationships. Agriculture must be developed from small-scale production to a modern agriculture based on production co-operatives able to utilise the latest machinery and techniques.

At present, the African peasantry is, in general, based on the petty ownership of the means of production, except in those parts where there is subsistence farming and a system of communal land ownership. In West Africa, the prevalence of small-scale commodity production is the core of the agrarian problem. In Ghana, 97 per cent of farms have a surface area of less than four hectares; and 60 per cent of them have less than two hectares. Small scale private farming is an obstacle to the spread of socialist ideas. It makes for conservatism and acquisitiveness and the development of a bourgeois mentality.

Under colonialism, and also in neocolonialist states, the government makes great use of the peasantry to form the rank and file of army and police. They are said to be "more loyal". In this, they exploit the illiteracy and qualities of submissiveness and conservatism characteristic of unawakened peasantry throughout the world.

During the national liberation struggle, the peasantry are pro-independence and against feudalism when they are led by political movements created in the towns by trade union leaders, workers and revolutionary intellectuals. For the peasantry, if it is to succeed in socialist revolutionary struggle, needs a class ally. In areas of the world where socialist revolutionary struggles have resulted in the successful overthrow of bourgeois governments—in China, Cuba, Vietnam, Korea—the peasantry, in alliance with other class forces, have been led by Marxist Parties. The close links between the proletariat and peasantry are analogous to the links between the urban and the rural guerilla. Each is an integral part of the socialist revolutionary struggle, and one cannot achieve final victory without the other.

In Africa, the socialist revolutionary struggle must be based on the peasantry and rural proletariat. They form the overwhelming majority of the population and their future lies with socialism. Freedom fighters operate in their midst, and are dependent on them for recruits and for supplies.

The countryside is the bastion of the revolution. It is the revolutionary battlefield in which the peasantry in alliance with their natural class allies—proletariat and revolutionary intelligentsia—are the driving force for socialist construction and transformation.

12

SOCIALIST REVOLUTION

The highest point of political action, when a revolution attains its excellence, is when the proletariat—comprising workers and peasants—under the leadership of a vanguard party the principles and motivations of which are based on scientific socialism, succeeds in overthrowing all other classes.

The basis of a revolution is created when the organic structure and conditions within a given society have aroused mass consent and mass desire for positive action to change or transform that society. While there is no hard and fast dogma for socialist revolution, because no two sets of historical conditions and circumstances are exactly alike, experience has shown that under conditions of class struggle, socialist revolution is impossible without the use of force. Revolutionary violence is a fundamental law in revolutionary struggles. The privileged will not, unless compelled, surrender power. They may grant reforms, but will not yield an inch when basic pillars of their entrenched positions are threatened. They can only be overthrown by violent revolutionary action.

Great historical advance is seldom, if ever, achieved without high cost in effort and lives; and those who argue that the transition from capitalism to socialism can be accomplished without the use of force are under a delusion. The qualitative change implicit in the socialist revolution is far more profound than that which was involved in the transition from feudalism to capitalism. Socialist revolutionaries seek a complete and fundamental transformation of society, and the total abolition of privileged classes; whereas the decline of feudalism merely ushered in a new stratification of society in which money, and not titles and land, became the basis of power and privilege. Socialist revolution opposes all concepts of elitism, and ends class antagonisms and racism. The socialist revolutionaries are fighting for a type of state which really expresses the aspirations of the masses, and which ensures their participation in every aspect of government.

Under capitalism, freedom is the right to do what the law permits, in the interests of the ruling bourgeois class. The more capitalism develops, the more anarchic it becomes; and socialist revolution is the logical and inevitable result.

Where capitalist development and industrialisation is in its infancy, and the bourgeoisie only represents a very small section of the population, socialist revolution can be achieved by workers and peasants seizing power by means of revolutionary action. Through socialist revolutionary leadership, Africa can proceed from bourgeois-capitalist ownership of property to arrive at socialist-communist ownership of property and the means of production and distribution. But in the revolutionary struggle, no reliance can be placed on any section of the bourgeoisie or petty bourgeoisie. Though these elements may join in revolutionary action during the struggle for national liberation, they will always, when it comes to the pinch, try to block the creation of a socialist state. They are committed to capitalism, and dependent for their very existence on the support of imperialism and neocolonialism. It is only when the bourgeois ruling class in neocolonialist states is overthrown by class-based socialist revolution, that fundamental changes in society can be accomplished.

Certain factors advance the process of socialist revolution. Foremost among them is capitalist development and industrialisation, which leads to an increase of urban workers—the sector of the population which generates the leadership of the proletarian revolution. Among other factors, are the desertion of the ruling class by the intellectuals; inefficient governmental machinery, and a politically-inept ruling bourgeois class. The example and the help of other socialist revolutions also assist the process. Finally, bitter class antagonism, and race-class problems, have the effect of accelerating the advance to socialism.

In the twentieth century, most forcible seizures of political power have occurred in areas of the world which have a relatively low level of industrialisation—namely areas which have a history of imperialism, colonialism and neocolonialism. These violent changes in the status quo cannot be explained in terms of the power struggles of elite groups. They represent actions of whole classes. In the case of socialist revolution, the seizure of power is by the working class; but in reactionary coups d'état, the bourgeoisie is further entrenched either by the ejection of a socialist-oriented government, or by a power struggle between different sections from within the existing bourgeois framework.

The economic, political and social ferment of Africa, Asia and Latin America, must be seen in the context of the world socialist revolution. For the world revolutionary process today unites three main streams: the socialist world system, the liberation movements of the peoples of Africa, Asia and Latin America, and the working class movement in the industrialised, capitalist countries.

The peoples of the less industrialised areas of the world are in a good strategic position to advance in the direction of socialist revolution as a result of their experience of imperialism, colonialism and neocolonialism. They see the issues clearly, since productive and distributive processes are not obscured or blurred by the trappings and diversions of the capitalist "welfare state", and capitalist corruption.

The cause of international proletarian revolution is part and parcel of the liberation struggles of the developing world. The class antagonisms in the contemporary world are highly concentrated in these areas. They have become the storm centres of world revolution, dealing direct and deadly blows at imperialism.

The embourgeoisement of certain sections of the international working class and the economism of socialist and working class leadership in some areas, has made the socialist revolutionary struggle in the developing world of even greater importance in

82

the world socialist revolutionary process. Thus, in some respects, the socialist revolutionary struggle has developed a class-race complexion. But while it would be harmful not to recognise the emergence of a racial factor in the revolutionary struggle, it must not be allowed to confuse or obscure the fundamental issue of socialist revolution, which is the class struggle.

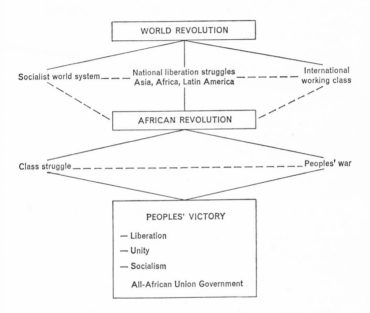

The developing world is not a homogeneous bloc opposed to imperialism. The concept of the "Third World" is illusory. At present, parts of it lie under imperialist domination. The struggle against imperialism takes place both within and outside the imperialist world. It is a struggle between socialism and capitalism, not between a so-called "Third World" and imperialism. Class struggle is fundamental in its analysis. Furthermore, it is not possible to build socialism in the developing world in isolation from the world socialist system.

CONCLUSION

The African Revolution, while still concentrating its main effort on the destruction of imperialism, colonialism and neo-colonialism, is aiming at the same time to bring about a radical transformation of society. It is no longer a question of whether African Independent States should pursue a capitalist or non-capitalist path of development. The choice has already been made by the workers and peasants of Africa. They have chosen liberation and unification; and this can only be achieved through armed struggle under socialist direction. For the political unification of Africa and socialism are synonymous. One cannot be achieved without the other.

"Peoples' capitalism", "enlightened capitalism", "class peace", "class harmony" are all bourgeois capitalist attempts to deceive the workers and peasants, and to poison their minds. A "non-capitalist road", pursued by a "united front of progressive forces", as some suggest, is not even practical politics in contemporary Africa. There are only two ways of development open to an Independent African State. Either it must remain under imperialist domination via capitalism and neo-colonialism; or it must pursue a socialist path by adopting the principles of scientific socialism. It is unrealistic to assert that because industrialisation is in its infancy, and a strong proletariat is only beginning to emerge, that it is not possible to establish a socialist state. History has shown how a relatively small proletariat, if it is well organised and led, can awaken the peasantry and trigger off socialist revolution. In a neo-colonialist situation, there is no half-way to socialism. Only policies of all-out socialism can end capitalist-imperialist exploitation.

Socialism can only be achieved through class struggle. In Africa, the internal enemy—the reactionary bourgeoisie—must be exposed as exploiters and parasites, and as collaborators with imperialists and neocolonialists on whom they largely depend for the maintenance of their positions of power and privilege. The African bourgeoisie provides a bridge for continued imperialist and neocolonialist domination and exploitation. The bridge must be destroyed. This can be done by worker-peasant solidarity organised and directed by a vanguard socialist revolutionary Party. When the indigenous bourgeoisie and imperialism and neocolonialism are defeated, both the internal and the external enemies of the African Revolution will have been overcome, and the aspirations of the African people fulfilled.

As in other areas of the world where socialist revolution is based largely on the peasantry, African revolutionary cadres have a tremendous task ahead of them. Urban and rural proletariat must be won to the revolution, and the revolution taken to the countryside. It is only when the peasantry have been politically awakened and won to the revolution that freedom fighters—on whom the revolution largely depends in the armed phase—will be able to develop and to expand their areas of operation. At the same time, the two main internal props of bourgeois power—the bureaucracy and the police and professional armed forces must be politicised.

The ultimate victory of the revolutionary forces depends on the ability of the socialist revolutionary Party to assess the class position in society, and to see which classes and groups are for, and which against, the revolution. The Party must be able to mobilise and direct the vast forces for socialist revolution already existing, and to awaken and stimulate the immense revolutionary potential which is at present lying dormant.

But as long as violence continues to be used against the African peoples, the Party cannot achieve its objectives without the use of all forms of political struggle, including armed struggle. If armed struggle is to be waged effectively, it also, like the Party, must be centrally organised and directed. An All-African Military High Command under the political direction of the All-African working class Party would then be able to plan unified strategy and tactics, and thus deliver the final blows at imperialism, colonialism, neocolonialism, and settler minority regimes.

Armed resistance is not a new phenomenon in Africa. For hundreds of years, Africans fought against colonialist intrusion though these heroic struggles have received scant attention in the histories of Africa compiled largely by foreign bourgeois writers. Indeed, it may be said that Africans have never ceased to resist imperialist penetration and domination, though the

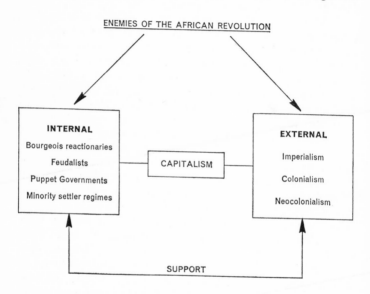

ENEMIES OF THE AFRICAN REVOLUTION

INTERNAL
Bourgeois reactionaries
Feudalists
Puppet Governments
Minority settler regimes

CAPITALISM

EXTERNAL
Imperialism
Colonialism
Neocolonialism

SUPPORT

resistance became for the most part non-violent as imperialism intensified its suppression and exploitation. For a time, when colonialism was in its hey-day, it seemed on the surface as though African resistance had been finally overcome, and that the continent would remain indefinitely under foreign economic and political domination. But resistance was always simmering just below the surface, and after the Second World War, re-emerged in a new active form in the struggles for national liberation. Though some of the liberation struggles

86

were accomplished successfully without resort to arms, others were achieved only after years of bitter fighting.

But political independence did not bring to an end economic oppression and exploitation. Nor did it end foreign political interference. The neocolonialist period begins when international monopoly finance capital, working through the indigenous bourgeoisie, attempts to secure an even tighter stranglehold over the economic life of the continent than was exercised during the colonial period.

Under neocolonialism a new form of violence is being used against the peoples of Africa. It takes the form of indirect political domination through the indigenous bourgeoisie and puppet governments teleguided and marionetted by neocolonialists; direct economic exploitation through an extension of the operations of giant interlocking corporations; and through all manner of other insidious ways such as the control of mass communications media, and ideological penetration.

In these circumstances, the need for armed struggle has arisen once more. For the liberation and unification of Africa cannot be achieved by consent, by moral precept or moral conquest. It is only through the resort to arms that Africa can rid itself once and for all of remaining vestiges of colonialism, and of imperialism and neocolonialism; and a socialist society be established in a free and united continent. In this the African masses have the support and assistance of the socialist world.

The African revolutionary struggle is not an isolated one. It not only forms part of the world socialist revolution, but must be seen in the context of the Black Revolution as a whole. In the U.S.A., the Caribbean, and wherever Africans* are oppressed, liberation struggles are being fought. In these areas, the Black man is in a condition of domestic colonialism, and suffers both on the grounds of class and of colour.

The core of the Black Revolution is in Africa, and until Africa is united under a socialist government, the Black man

* All peoples of African descent, whether they live in North or South America, the Caribbean, or in any other part of the world are Africans and belong to the African nation.

throughout the world lacks a national home. It is around the African peoples' struggles for liberation and unification that African or Black culture will take shape and substance. Africa is *one* continent, *one* people, and *one* nation. The notion that in order to have a nation it is necessary for there to be a common language, a common territory and a common culture, has failed to stand the test of time or the scrutiny of scientific definition of objective reality. Common territory, language and culture may in fact be present in a nation, but the existence of a nation does not necessarily imply the presence of all three. Common territory and language alone may form the basis of a nation. Similarly, common territory plus common culture may be the basis. In some cases, only one of the three applies. A state may exist on a multi-national basis. The community of economic life is the major feature within a nation, and it is the economy which holds together the people living in a territory. It is on this basis that the new Africans recognise themselves as potentially one nation, whose dominion is the entire African continent.

The total liberation and the unification of Africa under an All-African socialist government must be the primary objective of all Black revolutionaries throughout the world. It is an objective which, when achieved, will bring about the fulfilment of the aspirations of Africans and people of African descent everywhere. It will at the same time advance the triumph of the international socialist revolution, and the onward progress towards world communism, under which, every society is ordered on the principle of – from each according to his ability, to each according to his needs.

Index

93